The Curiosity Cycle: Preparing Your Child for the Ongoing Technological Explosion

Jonathan Mugan

Cover design by Val Toch.
Editing by Lynne Stair.

ISBN-13: 978-0692022122

Buda, Texas

Version 2.01

For Monica, Noah, Nathan, and Neala

Contents

Preface

Technology is rapidly changing our society, and this dynamic environment will provide opportunities for those with the flexible and adaptive thinking that come with curiosity. Creating curiosity is about creating anticipation. Novelists know this; they foreshadow events by giving hints of what is to come. Sports producers also know the value of curiosity. During the hype before the big game, they talk about the history of the teams and players, and they analyze how the players on the opposing teams match up to each other. Like novelists and sports producers, we have the ability to spark curiosity in our children. We can get them excited about the topics that will ensure their success and define their future.

In addition to being curious about the external world, children must understand how their internal emotional states affect their thoughts and behavior. They need to know that their own thinking is sometimes flawed and that impressions of the outside world can be distorted in their minds. Children also need to understand the social environment in which they are enveloped, and they must be able to recognize and predict the thought patterns of those around them. Compounding this complexity, our culture is increasingly being inhabited by smart machines, and our little social and emotional creatures must be adept at interacting with computers, which have alien thought patterns that are neither emotional nor social. Computers are becoming increasingly skilled at performing simple computations on the events and objects of real life, but they still need human creativity and curiosity to guide them. This book will help you to prepare your child to be mentally, emotionally, and socially ready for this environment.

Kids are under pressure to excel in school, and I believe that they spend too much time in the classroom learning how to do well on tests. The principles presented here will help your child achieve an intelligence that is broader than test scores. The goal is not to push kids harder, but to create a curiosity within them so that they are intrinsically and internally motivated to go out and acquire knowledge. The title of this book references curiosity instead of success or intelligence because the goal is to give children internally driven curiosity. Everything else follows naturally.

Is it even possible to teach a child to be curious? A recent book titled *Freakonomics* pointed out that activities such as taking kids to museums and reading to them are not enough to improve academic progress. The authors suggest that raising intellectually successful children is based on who you are, not what you do. I agree that taking kids to museums is not enough; I propose that it is *how* you take them to museums that matters. Vince Lombardi said: "Practice doesn't make perfect. Perfect practice makes perfect." It is not just about exposing your child to culture—it is *how* you expose your child to new ideas and *how* you interact with your child. The Curiosity Cycle points the direction toward that "how."

You will find that the approach I offer is different from most books about raising intellectual children. The principles presented here were developed while I was researching the question of how to build smart robots. My Ph.D. research was an interdisciplinary effort between robotics and developmental psychology, and I worked toward enabling robots to learn about the world in the same way that human children do. This research took me deep into the current literature on developmental psychology with the goal of developing a set of *actionable* principles that could be articulated and implemented on a robot. These principles form the foundation of this book. Children are not robots, but they both face the same problem of learning in complex environments. Viewing the minds of our children as computation machines provides insight that can make us better teachers.

This book targets parents of young children (from birth until about 10 years old), but my hope is that anyone interested in either human or artificial cognition will enjoy reading about the principles covered here. Where there was a trade-off to be made between scientific rigor and understandability, this book errs on the side of understandability.

I love thinking about our origins and watching the world change toward our unknown future. As our children move into this future, both the world and their roles within it will be constantly changing. This constant change means that the ability to learn will be more important than intelligence. My goal in this book is to show how children can become lifelong learners.

Chapter 1

Introduction

We learn by building models. Models enable us to understand the world and act within it, and our early models form the foundation upon which subsequent knowledge and skills are learned [87, 20, 70]. For example, after a child has mastered the skill of walking, that child soon learns the model that door knobs must be rotated to open doors. This model consists of the identified door knob and the rotation action needed to work it. On the way to mastering the skill of opening doors, the child will first learn an incomplete model that specifies only that door knobs are involved in opening doors without saying how. With this incomplete model, the child won't be able to reliably open doors, but the child will have just enough knowledge to be fascinated by them. It is these incomplete models that lead to curiosity.

Incomplete models are what motivates agents to explore and learn about the environment in computational theories of developmental learning [84]. If you know everything about a situation, there is nothing to learn and nothing about which to be curious. Conversely, if you know nothing about a situation, you can't make any sense of it and so will ignore it. When children ask why fire engines have sirens, we explain it to them, but they still only partially understand, and their models improve but remain incomplete. These incomplete models lead to a whole series of new questions, such as, "Why do the other cars need to get out of the way? Why do they have to get to the fire fast? Why? Why? Why?"

This book uses incomplete models to build a framework for thinking about curiosity called *the curiosity cycle*. In the curiosity cycle, children individuate concepts from the environment, such as door knobs and fire engines, and they use these concepts to build models, such as the model that door knobs open doors. Children then test these models to see how well they predict the environment, and through this process of testing, children learn new models and concepts leading to the next round of the cycle. For example, a child may try to open a door and find that it does not budge. This experience will lead to the new concept of a locked door. Further experience will show that a locked door can be opened if Mom or Dad has the key. In this way, new concepts lead to new models, and new models, by virtue of often being incomplete, lead to more curiosity.

The curiosity cycle, through the process of individuating concepts, building models, and testing models, allows children to construct a *web of knowledge* that encodes everything they know about the world. We can think of knowledge as a bunch of individuated concepts and a set of models that define the relationships between them. With the curiosity cycle, knowledge forms a web because the concepts are linked to each other through models, and the models are linked to each other through concepts that exist in multiple models.

A benefit of having knowledge organized in a web is that new knowledge can build on previously learned knowledge. Once children learn one thing, they can use that idea to learn other things. For example, a child quickly learns that the ringing of a telephone means someone is there waiting to talk. When this child moves into an office environment, the now young adult can build on that concept of ringing to learn that a ringing of the telephone that repeats two short rings indicates an outside call, and a ringing that repeats one long ring means an inside call. This model cannot be learned without first knowing the concept of ringing and then building on that concept to distinguish between repetitions of two short rings and one long ring. Trying to predict who might be calling raises a question that is partially answered by learning to distinguish between these two types of rings.

Using models to predict the environment is crucial to the curiosity cycle because testing improves models. Beyond improving models, the mindset of seeing the world through prediction has the benefit of allowing your child to view knowledge as tentative. Knowing that you might be wrong is the first step toward undoing an assumption and finding the right solution to a problem. Considering knowledge to be tentative cuts down on mistakes from not realizing that things could be another way. It leaves your child open to learning new things, and this can continue throughout life. Children must always be aware that some of what they know could be wrong—probably is.

A consequence of learning through prediction is that even an *incorrect* model is better than no model. We need models to predict the environment because models give us hypotheses to test, and the results of these tests allow us to learn. Of course, Mark Twain once said, "It ain't what you don't know that gets you into trouble. It's what you know for sure that just ain't so."[1] I believe this is true. When it comes to *decisions*, it is crucial to know that your model may not always be correct and to take that into account. But when it comes to *learning*, an incorrect model can be a useful place to start. We will also see in Chapter 3 that incorrect and incomplete models are also a good place to start when problem solving.

Another consequence of accepting incomplete models is that learning a little about something goes a long way. We have a tendency to avoid learning only a little about a topic, maybe because it makes us feel ignorant. But if we do learn even a little, we will have concepts and partial models that can keep accumulating over time as new information arrives. Without these partial models and concepts, we just ignore that incoming information and opportunities for learning are wasted. The result of the curiosity cycle is that the more your child knows, the more curious he or she becomes.

Learning through curiosity leads to adaptive thinking because your child is constantly trying to improve his or her models, and new ideas become embedded in the knowledge that your child already has. This type of learning means that your child doesn't just know facts by rote; he or she has models for why things are true and sees how they relate to everything else that he or she knows. These models can then be adapted when the situation changes. There is an old story [88] about a group of people in India who would trap monkeys using

---

[1] http://marktwainblog.org/

an emptied-out coconut filled with rice. The coconut had a hole that was large enough for a monkey to put its hand into but was too small for the monkey to pull its hand out with a fist full of rice. The trappers would attach this coconut to a stake. The monkey would come, put its hand into the coconut, and as the people came to capture it, the monkey would be trapped by its own brittle thinking. Its thinking was not adaptive enough to reevaluate the situation and realize that it should let go of the rice.

To further illustrate this idea of adaptive thinking, assume that x stands for the value of something in the environment that we care about, like the number of tacos in the refrigerator. Let's also say that your child and another child both know that $x = 8$. The other child has a shallow understanding and just has it memorized that $x = 8$. But if your child has a deeper understanding, he or she will have a model that determines where the value of x comes from, such as the simple model of $x = y + 3$, where y is the number of tacos delivered by truck and 3 is the number of tacos made on location each morning. Imagine that normally $y = 5$ because there are 5 tacos delivered by truck, but your child notices that the truck delivery y has increased by 1. Your child will instantly know that $x = 9$, but the other child will still think that $x = 8$. Also, your child will always be on the lookout for a better model, so if the world changes and the model $x = y + 3$ no longer holds on Saturdays, and now, on Saturday, $x = y + 6$, your child will notice and adapt his or her taco consumption accordingly.

As a more concrete example, I once took a linear algebra class in which everyone had done well on all the tests leading up to the final exam. Based only on previous experience, one would conclude that the final exam was going to be easy as well. But, by relating this information to other information, we know that not everyone can receive an A and the professor needs a separation of grades. Using this understanding, we come to the opposite conclusion: Since currently everyone is doing well in the class, and since there isn't much separation in the grades, the final exam will be especially difficult. It was.

In addition to enabling adaptive thinking, curiosity will enrich your child's life. Curiosity-driven learning makes learning more interesting because your child has a place to put new facts. Your child doesn't have to try to remember a bunch of unrelated ideas; everything fits together and is linked to what he or she already knows. Memorization is tedious, and it is easier to integrate new information when that information "makes sense" based on the concepts and models that your child already has.

To illustrate this point, consider the old experiment where both experienced chess players and novices were shown chess boards with pieces on them, and both groups were asked to later remember the locations of all the pieces [21, 94]. Experts performed better at remembering the locations of the pieces, presumably because they understood what they saw using their web of knowledge about chess. However, there was no difference between the groups in the ability to recall piece locations when the experiment used chess boards that were not from actual games (that is, when the pieces were just randomly placed on the board). In this case, the experts could not use their web of knowledge to interpret what they saw.

Each model that your child creates is like a little bet on how the world works, and these little wagers keep life entertaining. People who play fantasy football say that it adds another dimension to watching football games. You make a bet (by choosing who is on your fantasy team) and then see how it plays out. The little bets we make in life are often practical as well as entertaining, and air travel is one area where people enjoy pondering the many mysteries. For example, having an open seat next to me on flights is important so I can be comfortable and productive. I created a model that there are more open seats in the back of the plane because people generally prefer to sit up front to exit the plane faster. To test this model, I started sitting in back and found that indeed it does seem to improve the probability of having extra work space.

Besides making life richer, curiosity-based learning is internally directed and intrinsically motivated [83]. This internal focus means that we gain a sense of freedom from living this way. In school, your child will actually care about the subject being taught. Because the curiosity cycle is running, your child will want to use the subject material to help complete some of his or her models, much like a baseball card collector wants to complete a set. And because of this curiosity, it won't feel like work. Your child will feel like a free and natural human being doing what he or she wants to do.[2] This sense of freedom will continue into your child's career.

Curiosity can enrich our children's lives and endow them with adaptive thinking, but our children must also direct curiosity toward themselves as much as the outside world. Our brains are not perfect computation machines; they are organs with limited capacity for computation and memory, and they are subject to cognitive biases. Our children must learn how to properly use their brains

---

[2]There is a great discussion about being engaged in a subject you are learning about in school in *Zen and the Art of Motorcycle Maintenance* by Robert M. Pirsig.

so that they can recognize their biases and limitations. One of our limitations is that we are prone to cognitive laziness and reliance on instinct [49]. Going with our gut is often good enough, but our children need to learn that there are times when they must stop and think and actively use their brains. One such situation when self-reflection is called for is when we become emotional. During these times, self-awareness is critical to maintaining our equanimity.

Children also need to understand that our brains are coupled with our bodies in a unified system. The movement patterns of our bodies form the foundation of our knowledge [60], and this is partly why unstructured play is so important. Even mathematics is grounded in physical experience. We comprehend addition and subtraction as increases or decreases in the number of items in collections of objects [61]. Addition is adding items to the collection of teddy bears, and subtraction is reaching out and taking stuffed animals away.

Our children must also learn to continually examine the society in which they live and its affects on them. Sometimes, the effect of those around us is overwhelming. Later in the book, we will see that normal people like you and me are willing to administer dangerous levels of electric shock to innocent people just because an authority figure tells us to do so. In our everyday lives, companies exploit our cognitive weaknesses to sell us more and more, and fraudsters are particularly skilled at turning our own cognition against us.

To combat negative outside influences, our children need self-awareness and the ability to think for themselves. With the advance of new communication mediums surrounding the Internet, it is now increasingly difficult to shelter children from opinions that we find objectionable. Children must be able to filter the cacophony of voices in cyberspace to stay true to their own values.

Our children must also be prepared for the profound effect computers are having on our society. Unlike previous inventions, computers are more than machines that make particular tasks easier; they are general-purpose machines that can be programmed to do anything, and their usefulness is limited only by the creativity of the designer. This means that the success of our children will be determined in part by their ability to create new artifacts with computers.

The artifacts that our children create need not be physical because information is replacing physical goods as stores of value. The algorithms used to program computers are information, and even physical objects are now principally information. Prescription drugs are a good example of this. Sometimes you go to the register and it costs $4, and other times it costs $140. This disparity results because you are being charged for the information needed to make the pill, not the materials in the pill. This shift from physical objects toward information was first evident in documents. It used to be that documents were stored in filing cabinets, and electronic copies were just copies of the "real" document. But now it's the reverse; the permanent document is electronic, and we can create paper copies if we wish.[3] Continuing this trend, there are now 3D printers that can print physical objects such as bottle openers from information similar to how ink-jet

---

[3]Benjamin Kuipers pointed out this shift in documents to me.

printers print drafts of word processing documents.[4]

These changes brought by computers are reshaping the employment landscape. As they become more capable, computers will likely be able to do just about any job that does not require creativity. This eventuality adds extra urgency to the need for children to be able to think for themselves and become lifelong learners. On an even larger scale, these changes are reshaping how we live our lives. It is easy for us to be passive consumers because we are now bombarded with more entertainment options than ever. The ease with which we can live our lives in a perpetual state of entertainment means that our children are in danger of defining themselves as passive consumers instead of active creators. Curiosity can help your child avoid this quicksand.

---

[4]Last Christmas, our gift to my sister and her husband was a bottle opener printed on a 3D printer http://www.shapeways.com/model/321931/klein-bottle-opener.html.

Part I

Constructing Knowledge

Children construct knowledge by individuating concepts out of continuous experience and putting those concepts together into models that explain small pieces of the world. They continually test these models to see how well they predict events in the environment, and by identifying situations in which their models fail to predict experience, children can focus their natural concept-learning abilities to form new concepts that help them build yet more reliable models.

Constructing knowledge is more complicated than simply putting together available pieces of information because most of the world is hidden from view. Our environment is too big and interconnected for our perceptual system to show us everything. We feel like we see it all, but that is just an illusion. Consider the experience of learning the meaning of a new word. Once you learn that word, suddenly you see it everywhere. This is partly because words follow fashion like everything else, but the word probably didn't just pop into existence. It was there, and you were ignoring it without realizing it. The word was just background noise. Similarly, have you ever suddenly seen a new building on a familiar drive home? That building had always been there, but for some reason you never saw it before. The world is massive and continuous, but because our finite brains cannot possibly process all of it, we carve out what we need and ignore the rest.

We carve our experience out of the continuous world based on what we know. Our eyes do not work like video cameras [5]. Instead, they dart around from place to place, and using the bits and pieces we see combined with our background knowledge, our brain constructs an impression of the surrounding events. Once, I saw a cat while walking in a parking lot at dusk. I didn't wonder if I saw a cat. I saw a cat. But as I got closer, I recognized that it was in fact a beer bottle. If I had never had any experience with cats, I wouldn't have originally thought that I saw a cat, and my brain would have interpreted the beer bottle as something else. My brain constructed the image of the cat because it estimated that a cat was a likely thing to find at that location.

Because what we know determines what we see, learning new things changes how we experience the world [70, 45]. Consider trees: Before you learn about different types of trees, you only see generic trees when you look at the landscape. You might notice that some are big and some are small, and some have pointy needles and some have broad leaves, but for the most part they are just trees. Learning how to identify some trees changes what you see. You no longer look at the landscape and see trees; instead, you see live oak trees, southern magnolia trees, and cedar elms.

Part I of this book introduces *the curiosity cycle* to provide a framework for thinking about how we learn from our continuous sensory experience. Understanding how children construct knowledge through the curiosity cycle allows us to more effectively teach children how to learn from experience. After explaining the curiosity cycle, Part I turns its focus to how the curiosity cycle can be combined with problem solving to allow our children to better understand the wider world.

Chapter 2

The Curiosity Cycle

The curiosity cycle is a framework for understanding how children build knowledge. It consists of concepts, models, and tests of models. The *concepts* are the pieces that children pull from sensory experience, such as door knobs. The *models* specify how those pieces are put together to form useful information, such as how to open a door. And the *tests* are experiences that tell children how well their models work, such as trying to open a door and seeing that it works sometimes but not other times.

Testing can show models to be *incomplete*. An *incomplete* model is one that is partially formed but does not completely predict the environment. These incomplete models help children to form new concepts and to improve their models, for example by leading to the new concept that a door can be locked and the improved model that a door can only be opened if it is unlocked. Each new concept can be used in the current model, or it can become part of a completely new model, such as learning that windows can also be locked. In the curiosity cycle, curiosity comes from incomplete models because each such model gives the learner something to wonder about and a hole to fill.

The concepts, models, and tests are organized into a cycle as shown in Figure 2.1. Children have many curiosity cycles running simultaneously, allowing them to learn about doors, telephones, and everything else that is still only half understood in their environment.

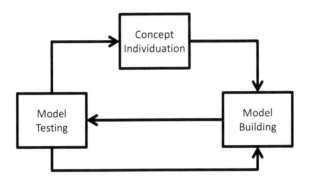

Figure 2.1: The curiosity cycle. Children individuate concepts from the environment, and they use these concepts to build models. They can then test these models to see how well they predict the environment. Through testing, children learn refined models and new concepts. These new concepts can lead to entirely new models.

2.1 Learning New Concepts

The first step to constructing knowledge is individuating concepts from the environment. Individuating concepts requires pulling cohesive pieces out of the continuous whole of experience. This process is so automatic that we don't realize we are constantly doing it. It feels like the concepts are just there to be seen, but this is not the case. Previously, I mentioned the example of trees. Consider another example: My wife and I were in a room, and she pointed out that the crown molding was beautiful. At that moment, I realized that I had never seen a crown molding before. I had heard the term "crown molding," and certainly my eyes had pointed in the direction of crown moldings before, but I had never before noticed it as a concept. And more importantly, I had never noticed that I hadn't noticed crown moldings. I didn't look at the top of a wall and think to myself that I didn't know what that thing was up there—they just didn't exist for me.

These elements and ideas that we individuate are *concepts*. A concept is something that you can think about consciously and can put a boundary around. A concept can be a person, place, thing, or idea. A chair is a concept. Talking loudly is a concept. Color is a concept. A concept can also be a feature of something such as "large" or "round" or "loud" or "heavy." A concept can also be a category such as "dog." We perceive the world in terms of concepts [70, 45].

Learning New Concepts by Building and Testing Models

Children can learn new concepts by building and testing models. A model is a small explanation about how something works, such as "turning knobs opens doors" or "rain makes roads slippery." Each model leads directly to a question: Does the model hold in this situation? Once that question is formed, your child's brain will pay attention to the environment looking for the answer. Sometimes the model will work, and that will be the end of it. But often, your child will find that the model doesn't always hold. In this case, he or she can pay attention to the environment and try to learn new concepts that make the model more reliable.

Let's consider in more detail the model that rain makes roads slippery. By paying attention to this model, you notice that the roads aren't always slippery when it rains, or that sometimes the roads are more slippery in the rain than other times. By paying more attention, you notice that the roads are more slippery when it rains for the first time in a long time and doesn't rain hard. You think about why that would be, and you remember that cars leak oil. You conclude that it must be that the oil accumulates on the road, and when it rains, all of the oil gets brought to the surface making the road slick. You now have a new concept that oil accumulates on roads over time and gets washed off by heavy and sustained rains.

As another example, I once learned the concept that rain gutters can signal the quality of construction for a house. In my neighborhood, there are houses built by two different builders, and the houses built by one builder are a little more expensive than the houses built by the other one. I was trying to predict which builder built each house, and I noticed that houses built by the expensive builder had gutters. In this case, it wasn't like discovering crown moldings, I knew what gutters were, but it had never occurred to me to use gutters as an indicator of quality of construction. Suddenly, my house looked naked without them.

New concepts can also be learned by comparisons

among objects. Given a group of objects, your child can try to discern which one is different, and how. It's that old song from *Sesame Street*, "one of these things is not like the others." Consider the following example. Your child notices that many trees lose their leaves in the fall, but also that some trees don't—some trees are not like the others. Your child calls these trees "evergreen trees" (or some other name, it doesn't matter which) and notices that they have needles. Now, putting aside the evergreens, your child is left with a group of flat-leaved trees that are each predicted to lose their leaves in the fall. Then, the child notices that there is a certain type of flat-leaved tree that does not lose its leaves in the fall—a live oak tree. It loses its leaves in March. Now the live oak tree is the one that is not like the others. It is doing its own thing.

Incidentally, this method of identifying the one that is not like the others is surprisingly effective on multiple-choice tests. In situations when only one thing should be chosen, it is probably the one that is not like the others. Indiana Jones knew this. He used this principle to correctly choose the Holy Grail in *The Last Crusade*.

Learning New Concepts by Learning from Others

In addition to learning new concepts by refining models, children learn new concepts directly from others. Parents and teachers point out new concepts to children all the time. We teach children about shapes, colors, body parts, categories of different animals, and the difference between trucks and cars. This is useful because the more concepts you can give a child "for free," the further the curiosity cycle can go. Of course, there is value in having a child figure things out independently because of the deep understanding acquired from this process. But there are plenty of concepts in the world, so you don't have to worry about your child running out of things to learn.

You should point out as many concepts to your children as you can. One core concept to focus on is the number of something. Instead of giving children a handful of blueberries, ask them how many blueberries they want.[1] If they request twenty, they learn a rough sense of how many twenty is. It is also beneficial to know the difference between volume and weight. To get your child familiar with weight, buy a scale and have your child weigh his or her toys. Similarly, buy a measuring tape so your child can become familiar with length and width. Another fundamental concept is direction. Have your child know which way is north at your home. Then, when out and about, randomly ask which direction you are traveling in.

It is also good to explain concepts in broader society, such as the role of money. Explain that we make money from working, we store it in a bank account, and we spend it to buy stuff. Ask what it would be like if, instead, we had to barter. More broadly, have your child think about the economy by considering alternatives. Can your child come up with other ways to get us to all work together? What problems might we have? For example, if your child comes up with the idea that we should just all work together for the common good, how do we make sure that everyone works hard? And how do we decide how many double-stuffed-crust pizzas to produce? Another

---

[1]Requiring children to name the number of food items they wanted was suggested to me by Maggie Myers.

good concept is where water comes from. Does the water in your house come from a well or a river? Similarly, talk about where electricity comes from.

Concepts that your child is not ready for can serve as placeholders. This applies even to things that you yourself do not understand. Consider that there are radio waves flowing through the air around you right now, and they somehow carry information! That's correct. Justin Beiber is in your house, even if you aren't listening to him at the moment. Amazingly, scientists have explained this (the radio waves, not Mr. Beiber) using equations that represent the laws of electricity and magnetism.[2] Imagine explaining to your children that such equations exist, and that they look so simple and explain so much. This explanation would give your child a "placeholder." Your child could then appreciate everything learned in math and physics as a stepping stone on the way to understanding this profound explanation.

This is probably a good time to point out that in this book I don't generally indicate which age a child should learn a particular concept. If your child is too young to fully understand a concept, he or she will still get something out of it and will also learn from the questions brought up by trying to understand it. We have all had the experience of "understanding" an idea multiple times. We first hear something and understand it, but then as we gain more experience, we understand it more profoundly. This can happen over and over again. You will find yourself explaining the same concepts repeatedly to your children over the years. These explanations are not wasted; they build little parts of models, and what is

---

[2]Maxwell's equations [93].

not understood can serve as placeholders.

It is also worthwhile to point out to your child the different ways that things can be organized. Teach your child about the hierarchical structure of category labels. For example, a Chihuahua is a type of dog, and a dog is a type of animal. By contrast, a bear is also a type of animal, but it is not a type of dog. A cycle is another way that things can be organized. One example of a cycle is the days of the week. Additionally, some things have a transitive structure. For example, if your child is older than the cat, and your cat is older than the dog, then your child is older than the dog.

2.2 Building Models

The next step is for your child to put the individuated concepts together into a *model*. A model is a linking of concepts into an understanding of how a small piece of the world works. Models can be used to predict the future, such as predicting that a certain person will talk loudly. Models can be causal models that show how the world changes. For example, consider an electric circuit with a switch, a light bulb, and a battery. Flipping the switch to close the circuit causes the electricity to flow through the wire and light up the bulb. This is a causal model because we see that if you cut the wire, the light bulb will go off. Models can also be observed patterns that predict the future but lack a causal mechanism to explain why that future comes about. For instance, in the late 1980s, rolling up your blue jeans in a certain way was correlated with being cool. I have no idea why.

Models are made from concepts. For the crown molding example, once the crown molding concept has been learned, your child can learn a model that says that if a building has crown molding, then the building is either fancy or old, or both. But without having the concept of crown molding, your child cannot build that model. Once a set of concepts is individuated, your child's natural model-building process can take over. If your child pays attention and has a desire to predict events, the models will emerge. In fact, it has been proposed that humans have an innate process for learning models [34], and it has been shown that human infants can detect contingencies (models where one event follows another) in their environment shortly after birth [25].

The rest of this section will discuss how you can encourage children to build models and improve them.

New Stimulation: Acting in Uncertain Environments

You can encourage children to build models by presenting them with new stimulation. Uncertain environments challenge us to build new understandings, and encouraging children to act in uncertain environments is about presenting opportunities and giving them the confidence to act and to possibly be wrong. Let your child lead the way. For example, when driving in a car, have your child navigate how to get home. Or have your child lead and determine what to do when you arrive at an airport. You could walk in and say, "Now what?" You may want to provide hints such as pointing out that the airline needs to know that you have bought a ticket. If you have bags to check, you hint that the airline needs to get them from you.

If you are not worried that a little knowledge can be

dangerous, let your child lead the way the next time you install software on your computer. Sit the child in front of the computer and ask what needs to be done first. Then talk him or her through the process of finding the software using a Web search and then downloading and installing it. This is also an opportune moment for you to talk to your child about malware (malicious computer programs such as viruses) and what can be trusted and what shouldn't be. (Chapter 10 addresses the issue of keeping kids safe online.)

You want your children to just dive right into new activities, such as learning new games and playing with new groups of kids. Let them know that it is okay to make mistakes, and praise them when they try something new. Children can learn just by being in new situations, and they can even learn when there is no explicit feedback [107]. The goal is to teach your children to be comfortable in uncertain environments.

Articulating Current Models

Encourage children to articulate their models as precisely as possible. Building and refining models is like pulling dinosaur fossils out of the ground. You initially need some insight to find the fossil because everything just looks like dirt. Once you have extracted the fossil, you still aren't done because it will be covered in chunks of dirt that obscure the finer details. The final step is to use your fossil brush to reveal the exact contours of the fossilized bone. Articulating a model is the equivalent of dusting off the fossil; it is getting rid of the extra stuff so you can see exactly what is there.

When a model just sits half-formed in your head, you

think it is complete when it may not be. By articulating the model, you find problems or deficiencies. One way to articulate a model is to describe it out loud to someone. Describing it out loud forces you to confront the parts of the model that feel complete but are not. Have your children describe their understanding of phenomena, and when they get older, have them write summaries of what was learned from particular experiences. These summaries should focus on what the child took away; they do not need to be complete or well written, but they should be in the child's own words.

Articulating models can also help us avoid thoughtless action. We seem to have this instinct to just start trying things, especially when we get frustrated. Once, a strap of my bag got caught in my car's trunk latch while I was rearranging some things. I immediately started pulling the strap in all directions to get it free, but it didn't work, and I started to worry that I was going to be late. Then, I stopped to think. It was trapped, and it looked like there was no way to free it unless I could somehow undo the latch. I looked, and there was no way to open the latch with my fingers. Suddenly, I felt relieved and silly. I put my key into the lock, opened up the latch, and freed the strap. (We will see in Part II that learning to stop and think can help us avoid cognitive biases.)

You want it to become second nature for your child to articulate exactly what is missing or not understood about a model or situation. When your child asks a question or doesn't understand something, have the child articulate exactly what he or she does not understand. Often, this process of articulating the exact question is enough to clear up confusion because it forces the child to examine the model and see where the holes are. It also forms a specific question for the child's brain to work on.

Generalizing Models

> *Knowledge is a process of piling up facts; wisdom lies in their simplification.*

— Martin H. Fischerl

In addition to articulating models, encourage children to generalize models so that they cover as many phenomena as possible. You want your child to always be looking for patterns and simpler, more accurate explanations of phenomena, and you want him or her to always be trying to classify things and situations into broader classes. Generalization is required for learning because without generalization, each event looks unique.

Generalization is the opposite of refining models and concepts. Consider the example discussed previously of learning which trees lose their leaves in the fall. That model was found by refining a general model to make it more specific. The child first believed that all trees lose their leaves in the fall. The child then added classes of exceptions to this model to finally arrive at the useful model that broad-leaved trees lose their leaves in the fall (except for live oak trees). By contrast, a child could start with a specific model and broaden it to arrive at a useful model. For example, the child could first notice that a specific tree in the front yard, a maple tree, loses its leaves in the fall. With this specific model, the child could then broaden the model when he or she found other kinds of trees that lose their leaves in the fall.

2.3 Testing Models

> *The most exciting phrase to hear in science, the one that heralds new discoveries, is not "Eureka!" (I found it!) but "That's funny..."*

— Isaac Asimov

We learn by being wrong. Models allow us to predict the future, and this prediction mechanism gives your child an opportunity to continually test the validity of his or her models. Crucially, models allow children to be wrong, and being wrong gives children an opportunity to improve their models.

A great thing about the world is that many of the questions we pose to it are answered as time unfolds. Each model that your child learns is like a scientific hypothesis and leads to the underlying question: Will the world unfold as the model predicts? This implicit question means that when children have a model that links together concepts, they can look to see if these concepts are actually linked in that way by observing events in the world. The response of the world allows children to refine the model or to individuate new concepts.[3] We saw this with the example of learning the model that trees lose their leaves in the fall. This model enables a child to learn about new kinds of trees because there are trees for which the model makes an incorrect prediction.

---

[3]Drescher [27] proposed a framework for learning multiple models and refining those models in an environment consisting of logical variables that could take on the values True or False.

As a breakfast-related example, there is an old joke that goes like this: What does "La Quinta" mean in Spanish? Answer: "Next to Denny's."[4] You might initially have a model specifying that Denny's restaurants are located near hotels. This model will often fail because you will frequently see hotels that do not have a Denny's next to them. But since you like Denny's (just go with me on this one) you try to make the model more reliable. One day, you notice that Denny's restaurants are more likely to be located next to a kind of hotel named La Quinta. Once you notice this type of hotel, you can identify it and find Denny's restaurants with increased reliability. By doing this, not only have you made your model more reliable, you have learned the new concept that there is a kind of hotel called La Quinta. Just like with trees, before you learned this concept, you only saw a generic hotel. Maybe you knew about four kinds of hotels, and your brain just mapped all others to "hotel." But now, La Quinta will be on your radar, and you will recognize a fifth kind of hotel.

Questions that Stump

You can encourage children to test models by asking questions that require them to use their models. This can seem boring, so make it a game. Try to stump your child by asking questions such as, "Which country is directly north of the United States?" Or, "If your TV show is 30 minutes long, how long would it take to watch it three times?" Or, "How long would it take to watch it one and a half times?" This is a perfect activity to do in the car. Your child will also try to stump you. My oldest son, who

[4]Jennifer Vespa Conway told me the Denny's joke.

was six at the time, and I were once playing this game. His question was, "What's my favorite kind of salamander?" I was stumped. I did not know his favorite kind of salamander. How many kinds of salamanders are there?

Guesses that Enlighten

One surprisingly effective technique to get children thinking is to encourage them to guess. Children are sometimes reluctant to answer for fear of being wrong, and guessing is a good way to have them test their models. A typical scenario is that you ask your child a question, and the response is "I don't know." When this happens, ask your child to take a guess and emphasize that it is okay if the guess is wrong. Often, the child will then actually consider the question and come up with a reasonable answer. Regardless of whether the guess is right or wrong, guessing makes your child use the model where just receiving the answer does not.

A great way to get children to guess is to tell them to predict the future. "Predicting the future" has a lovely ring to it that intrigues children. As a youth soccer coach, I use this technique and teach kids to predict the future by having them predict where the ball is going to go on a throw-in or kick. I teach them to guess where the ball is going to bounce out and to run to that location. The sky is the limit for anyone who can predict the future location of a soccer ball as it bounces around a dozen wild children.

Tips on Getting Started

At the end of each Chapter, I will provide some tips to help get you started using the principles described in that chapter. The following are some tips for encouraging children to identify concepts, build models, and test models.

- To help children acquire new concepts, always be looking for general concepts that you can explicitly point out. Even obvious concepts can sometimes escape notice. For example, you can point out that when people say goodbye they generally end with an agreement of when they will talk again. They say, "See you next Tuesday" or "I'll call you later" or sometimes just "See you later." Not only may the concept itself be useful, but having concepts explicitly pointed out to children will get them in the habit of looking for concepts themselves.
- To encourage children to form and refine models, pose questions that require children to make a prediction or a distinction. Ask them to look at the clouds to try to predict if it will rain that day. Or, ask them to try to predict if the school bus will be on time. Focus on finding new concepts that would help to make these predictions more reliable.
- Encourage children to guess if they become stuck on a problem or question. This lets them know that it is okay to be wrong and gets the creative process started.
- To identify new concepts, have your child tell you which object is different from the others when you encounter a group of objects.
- Have children articulate their understanding of phenomena in the environment and ask probing ques-

tions where their models appear fuzzy.

- Encourage children to test and refine their models by pointing out exceptions to their models. If your child believes that the mail comes on weekdays, point out that there are weekdays (holidays) when the mail does not come. This may lead to a new model: people do not work on holidays. This new model raises more opportunities for learning because it too contains many exceptions such as hospital workers and many restaurant workers.

Chapter 3

Learning by Solving Problems

Problem solving allows children to learn new concepts and models. For example, imagine that a child is playing with Legos and is trying to put wheels on a car using those individual wheels with holes in the middle. By solving this problem, a child can learn the new concept of "axle." He or she can also learn the new model that an axle can be used to attach wheels to a car. Problem solving also opens up avenues for exploration. After putting the wheels on the car with an axle, the child can then experiment with different configurations of the number of axles and wheels per axle.

Viewing the world through the lens of problems and solutions deepens our understanding of where we are and how far our civilization has come. Explain to your children that the structure of our society is the cumulative effect of solving many problems. This viewpoint helps children realize that the world hasn't always been the way it is now and that people just like them have made it what it is today. The problems that our children choose to work on will define their lives, and seeing the world as malleable will give them the self-confidence and perseverance to follow through.

3.1 Problem Solving Techniques

This section presents two basic problem solving techniques that you can teach your children. The first technique is to divide the problem into smaller pieces that are individually easier to solve. The second technique is to initially come up with an incomplete solution and then to improve it over time.

Divide and Conquer

Teach your child to look for ways to break down hard problems into multiple smaller ones. My four-year-old son once came to me asking for help to put a Lego arm back on an unusual Lego minifigure. This arm was strange because the hand and the connector that attached the arm to the body looked exactly the same, and at each end it could be attached in two different ways. This was actually two problems. The first problem was to find which of the four possible (two at each end) ways the arm could be attached. The second problem was how to apply the appropriate forces to get the arm on. Applying the right forces to put the arm on is easier once you are sure that you have the correct way to connect the arm.

Another example occurs in writing. It helps to break writing down into two problems: (1) what are you going to say; and (2) how are you going to say it. The first step can be accomplished by writing organized notes. When that is done, you can write the prose. Breaking down hard problems is also useful in math. It can be difficult for young children to solve problems like $21 + 19$. Be explicit and tell them to break this down by

1. Subtracting 1 from 21 to create the new problem $20 + 1 + 19$;

2. Adding 1 to 19 to create the new problem $20 + 20$; and

3. Solving $20 + 20$.

The best way to teach this method is to do it regularly with your kids. When you have a problem, or they come to you with a problem, think through it out loud with them and break it down.

Repeated Improvement

Another way to solve problems is to use an approach whereby the child first comes up with an imperfect solution and then refines it. As with learning incomplete models, coming up with something, anything, seems to help keep kids from getting stuck and gives them a place to start.

Consider again the problem of trying to put the Lego wheels on the car. Your child may initially have no idea how to put the wheels on. But to get started, your child can put a plastic rod in the center of both wheels, not because he or she understands that this will be part of the final solution, but because that rod is the only thing that fits in the wheels. Of course, this is not a complete solution because the rod is not attached to the car to serve as an axle. Your child will see that there is no way to attach the rod to the car with the wheels on, and may then remove the wheels and just focus on the rod. He or she will find that there are Lego pieces with holes in them for the rod to go through, and those pieces could be attached to the car. Then, your child can put the individual concepts together to get the wheels on the car.

The cartoon series *The Way Things Work* uses the concept of repeated improvement extensively. In each episode, a group of people living on an island has a problem, which usually involves the large group of mammoths that live with them. To solve their problem, they initially come up with an imperfect solution. But they keep refining their solution until eventually it works.

The results of repeated improvement are seen in products all around us. Looking at some advanced gadget, it feels like it must have been designed by geniuses. It is easy to forget that the first version probably didn't work well, and that it took a lot of people with a lot of ideas to get it working properly.

3.2   Problems to Understanding

Viewing civilization as the current set of solutions to a group of problems gives children an appreciation for the richness of society. Such a perspective also makes the world seem malleable and helps children to realize that society could be different. Some problems have yet to be solved, and these open problems can provide your child with a sense of wonder.

Problems As a Spark

Use problems as a spark for curiosity by telling your children stories about solutions that have already been found. One compelling topic for these stories is how early humans may have developed technologies. Since I have two boys and a girl, I make the stories about people like them. For example, you can make up a story of what it may have been like to discover and tame fire where the protagonists are two boys and a girl. As another example, you can introduce the topic of irrigation by telling a story about how one brother had some plants that needed water, so he carried buckets of water from the river to his plants. Then, his sister suggested digging a trench from the river to the plants so they could have more water and grow more plants.

These stories of discovery give children a sense of where modern society came from, and these stories also communicate that the world is theirs to be invented. Other topics you can tell stories about include inventing the wheel, the transition from iron to bronze to steel, irrigation, gun powder, the domestication of animals, the acquisition of dogs and cats as pets, and the energy transition from wood to coal to oil to nuclear to solar.

It might be worth doing a quick look-up on Wikipedia before telling a story on a topic, but the story does not have to be absolutely correct. In fact, for early discoveries, it's probably not even known how exactly they came about. I also tell stories about Neanderthals inventing various technologies even though Neanderthals probably didn't invent many of these things. The kids know that it was Homo sapiens and not the Neanderthals, but making it about Neanderthals seems to make it more appealing to them. The idea is to express the process of discovery—the transformation from not being able to do something to being able to do it. Describing discovery as a process gets children interested in history and helps them understand that anyone can shape the world.

Beyond teaching children that the world is malleable, we need to show them the magic of everyday life. Showing them this magic raises curiosity because it makes them reconsider their environment. It is amazing how things that we see every day don't seem amazing. If you were to walk up to a guy in the year 100 and tell him about boxes that play music by pulling invisible energy out of the air, you would be called nuts. But since radios are a part of our everyday lives, we don't think about them much. (Well, they used to be a part of our everyday lives.)

Consider the marvel of McDonald's. Imagine that you were talking to a caveman who had spent all day hunting a woolly mammoth with nothing to show for it but a broken arm and some bruised ribs. You tell him that there is this place where you walk in and order any food you want, as much as you want, and they give you the hot food you ordered, and then they thank you. Alternatively, imagine talking to a settler who had been traveling across the United States in a covered wagon on a trip that lasted for months. This settler saw half of her children die from disease and starvation. You tell her that last week you flew across the country in four hours. You go on to explain that it was a good flight but that it was a little uncomfortable because the guy in front of you reclined his seat. This idea is illustrated well by the comedian Louis C.K., who points out that it is odd to complain about the inconveniences of air travel when "you're sitting in a chair ... in the sky."

These are all examples of organizational and technological innovation. By understanding how far we have come, and all of the problems we have already solved, your children can get excited about all the advances that our society can yet achieve. Of course, the natural world is magical too. A seed is an incredible machine. It somehow converts dirt matter into a tree that can be 100 feet tall.[1] How does it do that? Other famous examples exist all around us, such as rainbows, and there are less-thought-about examples, such as skin. If you get a cut, the skin amazingly heals itself. It is like the new terminator in *Terminator 2*.

Ask Deep Questions

Asking deep questions is another way to unveil the magic. Ask your child crazy questions about the meaning of life and the origin of the universe. Scientists can trace the origin of the universe all the way back to the Big Bang—the huge explosion that started the universe in motion 13.7 billion years ago. Before the explosion, there was this incredibly dense ball of matter smaller than a grapefruit that contained everything in the universe [63]. How could that be? How did scientists come to the conclusion that the universe began that way? Even more amazing, where did this ball come from? What was there before the Big Bang?

Another great question to ask is if there is life on another planet besides Earth. We know that there are an

---

[1]In fact, it is even more astounding than that. Physicist Richard Feynman says that tree substance mostly comes out of the air! http://www.npr.org/blogs/krulwich/2012/09/25/161753383/trees-come-from-out-of-the-air-says-nobel-laureate-richard-feynman-really.

incomprehensible number of stars out there, and we are starting to see earth-like planets around some of those stars. Do any of them have life? If there is life on one of those planets, what does it look like? Movies show space aliens looking pretty much like us with two eyes and two arms and two legs, but it seems unlikely that they would be that similar to us.

On this planet, we are becoming more technologically advanced every year. Does your child think that we will ever colonize the galaxy? It seems likely that in a thousand years or so we will be ready to colonize our solar system and from there be ready to jump out and populate the rest of the Milky Way. A thousand years is nothing in the timescale of the universe. If there is life on other planets, and if it is natural that life would develop technology just as we have, then where are all of the space aliens?[2] Another great question to ask is whether time travel is possible. In the equations of physics, time can go in either direction [85], but just like with the aliens, if time travel is possible, where are all the people from the future?

Consciousness is another mystery. What does it feel like to be you? What does it feel like to be your child? Are dogs and cats conscious? It sure seems like they are. If so, what does it feel like to be a dog? What about a fish? Regardless of what you believe, these kinds of questions will generate fascinating discussions, and your child will learn that it is okay to ask questions that cannot yet be answered or even at all.

---

[2]The lack of visible space aliens is sometimes referred to as the Fermi paradox because it was pointed out by the physicist Enrico Fermi.

General Curiosity Techniques

There are many techniques you can use to instill curiosity through problem solving and through everyday interactions with your child. One technique is to embrace the whimsical and the absurd. Kids enjoy the absurd probably because children are more focused on exploration than are adults [37], and they consider more things to be possible. When picking the level of absurdity, you want something that is not likely but also not so unlikely that it doesn't make sense. You could tell them that cowboys used to ride on giraffes, but saying that cowboys used to ride on mice might be a bit of a stretch. (After the lesson, you will, of course, want to clear up any lingering misunderstandings as to the facts.) We will see in Part III that considering absurd possibilities is linked to creativity.

When I coach kinder soccer, I use whimsy to teach kids how to play. For instance, a fundamental skill in kinder soccer is being able to stay between the ball and the goal when playing defense. Staying between the ball and the goal sounds abstract to them, so to make the concept pop, I call the imaginary line between the ball and the goal the "magic line." During the game, I can tell them to stay on the magic line, and they know what I mean and are able to do it.

Kids need to know that the concepts under discussion actually exist. For example, it is less valuable to teach your child how to add fractions than to teach your child what fractions *are* and what problems they solve. Your child can use fractions every day when dividing up toys or pizza. By emphasizing to your child what fractions are and what they are good for, you ensure that when your child sees fractions formally introduced in school, he or she will already be interested in them. This does not mean, of course, that you shouldn't teach your child how to add fractions, but fractions should be incorporated into everyday life so that when he or she does learn to add fractions, either at home or in school, it makes sense and is seen as a useful tool.

When your child learns something new, point out that new thing wherever you see it. If your child sees a video on punctuation, point out the punctuation when you are reading to the child. Also, when trying to make an idea important in your child's mind, reference his or her favorite movies and TV shows.

Children need to know why they are learning something, and the best case is when learning is directed from within. An ideal situation would be that your child realizes that he or she needs to know how to do x in order to solve a problem that you two are working on together. Once this happens, your child is motivated to learn x. This is opposed to just teaching about x. Integrate this type of learning into your daily life. When you play basketball, keep score, and have the child figure out the current score. The same goes for playing football; your child can learn to count by sevens this way. Or, when you are loading a computer program and it says "30% loaded," teach your child about percentages. One phrase that I've found to be particularly useful is, "I'm going to show you something."

Another technique to get kids (young ones anyway) to do something or be interested in something is to do it yourself. It is hard to get kids interested in things by telling them to be interested; if you want them to watch nature videos, you can sit down and watch nature videos. They will ask to join you, and later they will be more likely to watch nature videos on their own. In my house, if I tell my oldest son to play or practice piano, he doesn't want to, but if I sit down and start playing, suddenly he wants to join.

Another curiosity technique is to let excitement spill from one topic to another. Use the child's interest in one subject to spark interest in other subjects. Your child may go through phases of intense interest in a particular topic such as dinosaurs, princesses, or the solar system. Encourage this, and also use it as an opportunity to incorporate other subjects such as math and geography that are related to the topic of interest.

If your child loves princesses, talk about politics and how countries choose leaders. Discuss how marriages were often arranged to solve the problem of forming alliances between regions. If your kid loves dinosaurs, use dinosaurs to talk about biologically related topics such as the composition of the atmosphere, how lungs work, the food that each dinosaur ate, what it means to be nocturnal, and different defense mechanisms of the dinosaurs. Continuing with the dinosaur example, if your child loves *Tyrannosaurus rex*, you could spark an interest in geography by finding places on a map of the world where *Tyrannosaurus rex* bones have been found. Here again, it is okay if you don't know these things yourself. A crucial skill of curiosity-based learning is the ability to be comfortable in a new area, and there is no better way to teach this skill to your children than by letting them observe you in situations when you don't have all of the answers but are still willing to discuss, learn, and raise questions.

3.3 Choosing Problems and Following Through

Problems are often encountered as barriers between us and our goals, and since problems provide opportunities for learning, the goals that we set will determine what we learn and ultimately who we become.

Setting Good Goals

We need good goals because it's a waste of time to work hard climbing a ladder that's against the wrong building. A good goal is one that leads to a fruitful result and is within your child's control. The benefit of a good goal can either come from valuable learning that occurs while achieving the goal or from a result itself that is somehow useful. This requirement that the result be useful is what often makes video games a waste of time. When immersed in the game, we feel like we are making progress and working toward a useful result, but that result has no meaning in the real world.

Setting a lofty goal with a potentially large benefit can teach a child how much work is necessary to be great at something, even if the child does not succeed, but it is worth bearing in mind that not all goals are within the child's power to achieve. Playing professional baseball may not be a good goal because there is too much chance involved.[3] Many people do all the right things and work hard but never make it because of injury or not having enough innate ability. Getting into a specific

---

[3]There was a good discussion in the book *Freakonomics* [65] about how some professions are like tournaments. Not many people can make it, but the prize is great.

school like Harvard also requires luck. Harvard receives more qualified applicants than the number of open positions. By contrast, a good goal may be to be a good baseball player, to improve one's hitting, or to get into a quality university. These are under your child's control.

Likewise, being valedictorian may not be a good goal. Too many things outside your child's control, such as being sick on the day of a deadline or the whims of the graders, can interfere. Ironically, by being overly focused on grades, your child could sacrifice learning. Learning sometimes will take your child off the path of assigned coursework. This is to be encouraged. Your child should aim high and have high expectations, but don't be overly rigid about the path that he or she should take. Instead, encourage your children to create their own goals and to maintain the flexibility needed to go after previously unforeseen opportunities.

Working on a goal often creates a feeling of "flow" [23]. Flow leads to happiness and comes from being in the moment and being directly engaged with a task. A good task for flow is one that is well defined with a clear path to completion and for which it is possible to measure progress. Additionally, the task should not be too hard or too easy. Video games are designed to exploit our psychological desire for flow, and this is why it feels like we've achieved something when we earn the next super weapon to kill the next level of monsters. While I am hard on video games, they can teach us much by placing us in new environments and in other people's shoes, and in Chapter 10 we will see that there are games that allow your child to create.

Perseverance

> *The very little engine looked up and saw the tears in the dolls' eyes. And she thought of the good little boys and girls on the other side of the mountain who would not have any toys or good food unless she helped. Then she said, "I think I can. I think I can. I think I can." And she hitched herself to the little train.*
>
> — Watty Piper, *The Little Engine That Could*

Perseverance comes form self-efficacy. Self-efficacy is the belief that you can change your environment if you try, and it is built by success on tasks [6]. Self-efficacy stimulates curiosity because believing that their actions can change the world makes children more likely to take on challenging goals and to continue through in the face of difficulties.

To build self-efficacy, you want to set up the situation so that your child can succeed, but you don't want too much easy success. You want to instill that success comes from hard work and is within your child's control. One of my psychology professors once told us that the best thing that can happen to you is success in the context of failure.[4] He also said that the worst thing that can happen to you is failure in the context of success.

Success in the context of failure teaches your child to work through adversity. When my son started first grade

---

[4]Jack Nation, psychology of learning class, Texas A&M University.

he had trouble making friends because all of the boys in his class were neighbors and already knew each other. But as the year went on, he did make friends. This was a valuable experience because at first he had trouble, but by continuing to try, he was able to overcome. By contrast, failure in the context of success can teach your child that it is useless to try. For example, my son was having a successful basketball season up until the last two games. Because the court was built on top of an ancient burial ground, or some other equivalent reason, all of his shots in those last two games would bounce promisingly around on the rim but would not fall. It was heartbreaking, and doubly so since it was the last two games of the season and he had been doing so well. It took him a long time to want to play basketball again. However, if he'd had his bad luck at the beginning of the season and finished with success, it would have actually been a positive experience.

Success in the classroom seems to be particularly affected by self-efficacy. We need to teach kids that intelligence is something they grow, not something they are born with.[5] Encourage their effort, don't just say they are smart. Kids who are told they are smart are apt to give up when they see a hard problem because they do not want to shatter their self-esteem. If you drill into kids that practice is required, they won't be so quick to give up when difficulties arise.

---

[5]The ideas in this paragraph come from Stanford professor Carol Dweck. See her excellent article in *Scientific American Mind* [29].

Tips on Getting Started

Here are some tips on helping your child better understand the world through problems and solutions.

- When your child asks you to solve a math problem, such as figuring out the sales tax on an item, work them through the two problem-solving methods described in the chapter. If the item is priced as $1.50, you can use divide and conquer. First figure out the tax on $1.00, then take half of that and add it in to get the tax on $1.50. You can also use repeated improvement. If the item costs $9.00, first calculate the tax on $10.00. This is close, and you can improve it by subtracting the tax on $1.00.

- Point out solved problems in your everyday environment to your children, even if you do not know how they were solved. For example, how do they get the water and electricity to our houses, and how do they know how much we have used?

- Ask your child to ponder unusual problems and questions that come into your head. For example, you could ask your child, "Which is more complicated, all of the hardware and software on our laptop computer or a biological cell?"

- When your child asks how a system works, like credit cards, ask him or her to tell you what problem it is solving. Then, ask your child how he or she would solve that problem.

- To teach your children to persevere, constantly remind them that they get better at things through "practice, practice, practice." When they comment that someone is great at something, highlight that he or she got that way through practice.

Chapter 4

Understanding Our Civilization through History, Mathematics, and Language

In this chapter, we continue our exploration of society through solved problems by focusing on history, mathematics, and language. History consists of a sequence of events, and knowing the sequence of events that led to the current state of the world gives our children significant insight into its structure. This insight helps children to understand the present and to predict the future. A different kind of understanding of structure can be obtained through mathematics. Mathematics expresses profound truths about the nature of reality [109], and it is the tool that is building our future. Language is how we communicate our understanding of reality. It binds us together and enables us to pool our resources and brainpower by providing a mechanism for transporting ideas from one person's head to another's.

4.1 History: Using the Past to Understand the Present

To be ready for the future, your child must understand the present by being curious about the past. Get your children interested in the big soap opera that we live in by telling them about it in ways that they can understand and relate to. Discuss problems that our society faces and then work through possible solutions together.

Anticipation: Following the Soap Operas

Knowledge of history makes us excited about what comes next, just like in a soap opera. We love a story that unfolds over time, and we continue to pay attention to see how it will play out. As mentioned in the preface, sports promoters are masters at this. Before the game, they give the viewers a tour of the history of the teams and the key players. This same approach is used by news organizations to promote politics. The election coverage is more about how new developments will help or hurt a candidate's chances than it is about the issues. Just like with sports, it's a big reality show.

You can use the soap-opera technique to get your child interested in the processes shaping society. Consider global energy consumption. Some books and documentaries argue that the world is running out of oil and we are heading for societal collapse [58, 33]. They begin by explaining that oil is used not only for transportation, but also for essential products such as plastics and fertilizers. From there, they argue that oil is a uniquely cheap and convenient energy source that has enabled our technological development. They point out that gasoline that costs over $4 a gallon seems expensive but is actually downright cheap when you consider that Starbucks coffee costs around $30 a gallon. To bring the point home, they note that one cup of gasoline, which costs 25 cents, will transport you and a few friends more than two miles (as well as a car that weighs 2,500 pounds).[1]

After convincing you that oil is a requirement for society and that we take cheap and plentiful oil for granted, they argue that we are starting to run out. They point out that most of the earth has been scoured for oil and assert that all of the large pools of oil have already been found and exploited. They then present evidence that oil output from existing fields is declining because those fields are running dry. They call this "peak oil." Regardless of whether you believe this or not, if you are following the news about global energy reserves, then stories about new sources such as methane hydrates or new technologies such as hydraulic fracturing (fracking) are not just background noise to be ignored, they're entertaining.

You can also use the soap opera technique with science. You and your child can follow the progress of the Large Hadron Collider (LHC). The LHC is a massive scientific experiment going on at the border between France and Switzerland. The goal of the LHC is to smash particles together to see if the collisions can help answer funda-

---

[1]Calculation for 25 cents to transport you two miles: There are 16 cups in a gallon. If gasoline is $4 a gallon, then 25 cents is 1/16 of a gallon, and assume 37 miles per gallon highway.

mental questions about the structure of space and time. As with science, creating anticipation to see how the story will unfold also works to raise interest in technology. If you are following the number of pixels that are available on a TV screen, it can be exciting to watch that number grow as new models of TVs come out.

The obvious generalization is to see our whole history and culture as one giant soap opera. If you follow European history and how Europeans started using the euro as their currency, it becomes interesting to read about the current difficulties of maintaining a single currency across disparate economies. Another example is the situation with oil in Mexico. The Mexican government receives around 30 to 40 percent of its revenue from oil exports, but they are having increasing trouble maintaining production [56]. Despite this, they will not allow foreign oil companies with the needed expertise to extract the remaining oil. This behavior makes more sense if you know the history of countries regretting giving too much power to foreign oil companies.

To create interest in current events, tell stories about real events in the past such as landing on the moon or the Civil War. Don't worry about exact dates or names, just make it compelling by focusing on what it might have been like to be involved. You can also raise interest in current events by discussing and being engaged in them in your home. When a new president is elected, let your child stay up late to watch the acceptance speech. Happy or sad, you can order pizza and make it special. As we saw in Chapter 2, even if your child is too young to understand what is going on, new model fragments and concepts will start to accumulate.

Problems to Progress

We saw in the last chapter that problems and solutions lead to transformations in how your child sees the world and can open up avenues for future exploration. Likewise, if we think about the problems that led to our institutions, we can more deeply understand those institutions.

Thomas Hobbes famously said that without government, the natural state of human life is "nasty, brutish, and short" [43]. We need to work together to create a society where everyone can prosper. To do this, we must determine how to build and manage shared resources, such as roads and bridges. Yet, each individual is motivated to maximize his or her own access to resources. Given these competing goals, how can we work together? If you think about government as a solution (although imperfect) to a problem, learning about the government suddenly seems less dry.

Explain to your child how institutions like banks work using simple stories. For instance, Bob is a farmer, and he is getting ready to plant. Bob needs to buy seed to start planting, but he doesn't have any money, and he won't get any money until later when he sells his crops. Bob could find someone to loan him the money, but who? Sally lives in town, and she has money. Sally doesn't need anything at the moment, and she doesn't want her money to lose value to inflation or risk putting it under the mattress. How can Bob and Sally find each other? Even if Sally and Bob can find each other on an online message board, how can Sally trust that Bob will pay the money back? And what if, after loaning the money, Sally suddenly needs it for an emergency?[2]

Let your child think about this problem for a few moments and start to come up with ideas. Together, talk about those ideas and refine them. Eventually, you may work your way toward an idea for an institution that looks a lot like a bank. Bob gets a loan from the bank and Sally deposits money in the bank. The bank has many depositors and borrowers, like Sally and Bob, at the same time. This way, Sally and Bob do not have to trust or even know each other.

We saw the example of money as a concept that you can point out to your child, and we saw how we can even think of the whole economy as a problem and capitalism as our solution. Ask your child what would happen if a fundamental part of our economy changed. For instance, what would happen if people who owned companies no longer needed human workers because robots could do all of the work? If this occurred, people wouldn't have jobs. If people didn't have jobs, who would have money to buy the stuff the company makes? In this case, we might need a new system. What would it be?

4.2 Mathematics: A Useful and Fascinating Game

Math is both abstract and practical, and it has clear rules and answers that are unambiguously right or wrong, which makes it a fun game. Another way to describe math

---

[2]There is a relatively new phenomenon called peer-to-peer lending where Sally and Bob do try to find each other directly. You can read more here `http://www.mrmoneymustache.com/2012/09/24/th e-lending-club-experiment`.

is to say that it is an abstraction that lets you do stuff. The equation $2 + 2 = 4$ could mean that two blocks plus two blocks makes four blocks, or it could mean that if you have two tacos and you buy two more, you have four tacos. In this way, math helps us to reason about the physical world.

There are still many unsolved problems in mathematics. To spark interest, tell your child that he or she can win a million dollars by solving one of the famous open math problems[3] and that he or she can win cash prizes by winning a math competition.[4] Your child won't be able to dive right in, but having the knowledge that there are such prizes can spark interest and curiosity. You see professional football players making big money, why not mathematicians? Of course, the chance of your child solving one of these particular problems is small, but there are certainly more millionaires in the world who were trained in math and science than who earned their millions by playing professional sports.

Math is the language of our machines and the driver of our technological explosion. Math is also the language needed for understanding the data that our machines create as they observe us and themselves. The discipline created to sift through this data is called data science, and it is one of the most exciting careers of this century [75].

---

[3]http://www.claymath.org/millennium-problems/millennium-prize-problems and http://www.claymath.org/millennium-problems

[4]http://www.kaggle.com/competitions

Making Math Concrete

I emphasized earlier that kids need to know that the concepts you are teaching them actually exist; this is especially true in the abstract domain of mathematics. Counting is one of the first and oldest technologies that your child will learn. The first counting was probably done with notches on bone or wood to count animals. Each number is a symbol: the number 5 symbolizes five notches on the bone.

To teach your child to count, always ask the child "How many?" This reinforces the idea that the number of something is a fundamental concept. When kids are young, three to five years old, you can gather 100 objects (make sure they are not a choking hazard), and play little games where you put them into groups of 10.

To learn addition and subtraction, have your kids count on their fingers. Counting on their fingers and counting using real objects is valuable because we want the child to have a deep understanding of what addition and subtraction *are*. It is less important that they come up with the answer; what is important is the understanding. There is no need to teach your child to memorize $2 + 2 = 4$. Memorization should come as a shortcut *after* your child has learned what addition is. You can also have your children buy imaginary items and play games with coins that require making change.

Multiplication and division are about groups of objects. You can teach this by grouping and regrouping objects. For example, lay out six items before your child. Count them together, and point out that this group can also be looked at as three groups of two or as two groups of three.

Incorporate math into everyday problems. Like with the stump game, ask questions such as, "If we have three 13-minute videos, how long does it take to watch all three?" Show your child that solving the problem itself is fun. Also have your child guess how many there are of something, count them together, and have him or her tell you how many would be left if half were removed.

After you make numbers concrete, you can move to *sequences*. Explain to your child that a sequence is a list of things in order. Sequences are all around us. A word is a sequence of letters, and a phone number is a sequence of numbers. Music is a sequence of notes. Give your child the first part of a sequence and see if he or she can guess the rest. In an arithmetic sequence, each next number is greater than the last by a fixed amount. For example, give your child 3, 7, 11, 15 and see if he or she can guess the next number. In a geometric sequence, each next number is greater than the last by a fixed ratio. See if your child can guess the next value in the sequence 2, 4, 8, 16. Some sequences are famous in mathematics, such as the Fibonacci sequence. The first eight numbers of the Fibonacci sequence are 0, 1, 1, 2, 3, 5, 8, 13. See if your child can guess the structure of this sequence and guess the next number.

Making shape concrete is what led to geometry. Geometry is the study of size and shape [67]. Have your child go around and point out all the crazy shapes in the room or outdoors. Then teach him or her to calculate the area of a square and rectangle and demonstrate that the area of a triangle is half of that.

You also want your child to be comfortable with the idea of a *variable*, which is often introduced during the study of algebra. Algebra is used to represent relationships. If a soccer ball always costs five dollars more than a football, if you know the price of a football, you can know the price of a soccer ball.[5]

$$\text{price of soccer ball} = \text{price of football} + 5$$

Of course, in the algebra that we are used to seeing, the variable names are shorter and less descriptive, such as x and y.

Start your child off with simple equations so that the notation doesn't seem so weird when it is first encountered in school. To do this, show your child the progression

$$
\begin{aligned}
4 + 2 &= ? \\
4 + ? &= 6 \\
4 + x &= 6
\end{aligned}
$$

where, initially, "?" stands for the unknown and appears on the right side of the equal sign so it is intuitive. Then, you move "?" to the left side of the equal sign. And finally, you replace "?" with x and you have a standard equation from school.

Once your child understands the basic notation for equations, you can also start to demonstrate some general concepts in mathematics. For example, demonstrate that $x + y = y + x$ for any value of x and y. Do this by getting two sets of objects, toys or whatever, and assigning the number of objects in one set to x and the number of objects in the other set to y. Then you can just start

---

[5]The description of algebra is inspired from [101]. Steven Strogatz is a mathematician who can explain things beautifully to non-mathematicians.

counting them, and you see that it doesn't matter if you start counting with the x set or the y set, you get the same number of objects. You can also demonstrate that $x \times y = y \times x$ by drawing a bunch of dots in the shape of a rectangle with x rows and y columns. Show that it is the same number of dots even if you rotate the rectangle by 90 degrees.

Math and the Machines

Our machines are made of math, and one of the simplest machines is a function. A function is a mapping from one list to another. If you give a function an input, it provides the output. Just like guessing the next value in a sequence, you can have your child guess the function you are thinking of. In your head, you could have the function $f(x) = x + 5$. In this case, $f(x)$ means that for whatever value of x that your child gives, you give that value plus five. Have your child give you a number, like "17," and you say "22." After a few iterations, probably before, your child will guess the function, and then you can go on to the next one.

You can also create functions from one kind of thing to another. For example, tell your child to give you a letter, and you then tell the child a number. If your child says "K," then you can say "11." If your child says "A," you can say "1." Your child will get that each letter corresponds to its position in the alphabet. Then ask your child to give you a word. If your child says "cat," you can mentally add $3 + 1 + 20$ and say "24". Then if your child says "potato," you, after locating a piece of paper and a pen, can say "87." Your child will enjoy making up functions and trying to stump you.

Functions have two steps: (1) You provide the input; and (2) they provide the output. An *algorithm* is a recipe for doing something that consists of a *sequence* of steps. When you bake a cake, you are following the steps and running the cake-producing algorithm. The sequence of steps in an algorithm does not have to be fixed as it does with a recipe, it can depend on the situation. When you do addition by hand, you are running an algorithm. Addition by hand (at least the old way we were taught in school) is a little different from baking a cake because what you do at a particular step is conditional on the state of the problem. *If* the rightmost digits you are adding sum to 10 or greater (for example, 6 + 7), *then* you will have to carry a 1; *otherwise*, you don't carry a 1. You even run an algorithm when you fill a glass of water. *First* you turn on the faucet, *then* you hold the glass under the faucet *until* the glass is full.

An algorithm is a good concept for your child to know because the terms *sequence, if, then, otherwise,* and *until* are useful ways to think about actions and instructions. In fact, when we think of algorithms, we usually think of computer programming. Computer programming is the process of communicating an algorithm to a machine. In the future, programming will be done by more people than just computer programmers because we will all engage in some form of programming when we interact with semi-intelligent objects, as will be discussed in Part III.

Algorithms can be used to encode the rules of *logic* to create a little machine that decides what must be true. Logic does not come naturally to us; it needs to be learned [71], but you can teach logical thinking to children. We have all heard the argument, "All men are mortal. Socrates was a man. Therefore, Socrates must have been mortal." You can make this kind of syllogism fun for kids. You could say, "All dinosaurs are happy. Frank is a dinosaur. Is Frank happy?" Your child will say "yes." Then you could say, "All dinosaurs are happy. Bob is happy. Is Bob a dinosaur?" Again, your child might say "yes." Explain that in this case, we do not know that Bob is a dinosaur. You can provide a counterexample and say, "I am happy, but I'm not a dinosaur."

You can even use this method to introduce your child to the technique of *proof by contradiction*, which is a method for proving that something must be true by showing that its opposite would be absurd. Specifically, a statement can be proven true if it can be shown that the statement being false would lead to a contradiction with something that we already know to be true. To demonstrate this, you could say, "Being green makes a dinosaur sad. Tom is a happy dinosaur. Is Tom green?" You then point out that we know Tom cannot be green, because since Tom is a dinosaur, if he were green, we would have a contradiction with the assertion that Tom is happy.

Logic is a powerful tool, but much of the world appears random. Explain to your child that something is *random* if you can't predict what is going to happen. Challenge your child to roll a die and to predict what the value will be. Sometimes, the prediction will be correct, but roughly five out of six times your child will be wrong. Explain that even when you don't know what is going to happen, some events are more likely than others. For instance, we don't know if a bazooka will be on your child's school supply list for next year, but it seems unlikely. Similarly, when we roll a die, we don't know if the number that comes up will be less than 3, but it probably won't (although that is a significantly more likely event than the requirement that each child come to school armed with a man-portable antitank weapon, even in my native Texas).

The *probability* of an event is the chance that it will occur. For example, the probability that a roll of a die will come up with five is 1/6, and the probability that a coin flip will come up heads is 1/2. The beauty of probability is that it is just common sense reduced to calculation.[6] Consider the idea of *expected value*, which takes the value of each possible outcome and multiplies it by the probability that it will occur. It then sums up all of these products to give the value that you would expect to get from some future event. This is best shown with an example. Imagine a game where you flip a coin, and if the coin comes up heads, you get $10, and if it comes up tails, you get $2. In this case, the expected value of this flip is $6 = (0.5 × $10) + (0.5 × $2). Using the concept of expected value, your child can figure out how valuable it is to enter a drawing or lottery. For example, if a $500 iPad is being given away, and 10,000 people enter, the expected value of entering the contest is five cents. It is not even worth filling out the form. As always, the term "expected value" itself is not important, the concept is important. If "expected value" doesn't resonate with your child, call it something else like "what you expect to get."

When talking about probability, the *state space* is the set of all possible ways the outcome can be—either you win the iPad or you don't. If you flip a coin, the state space is heads or tails. If you roll two dice, one after the other, the state space is all of the possible outcomes and

---

[6]The statement that probability is just common sense reduced to calculation is attributed to Pierre-Simon Laplace.

is of size $6 \times 6 = 36$. The state space of the world is a powerful concept that we will see in Part III. It is tied to how computers think, and it is even tied to creativity.

Math, Problems, and Estimates

Math is often taught to our children as if they were machines, but as we will see in Part II, our brains have significant strengths and limitations compared with actual machines. Kids spend a lot of time in school learning how to get the exact answer to math problems using the pencil-and-paper algorithms for addition, subtraction, multiplication, and division. It is useful for children to know these algorithms, but it is the concepts that really matter.

When teaching your child math, you want to separate the algorithm from the concrete concept. In school, the algorithm and the concept are often taught together as one thing. For example, division is not the algorithm for long division, that horrible, error-prone process; it is a way for dividing objects into equal-sized groups. Even the relatively simple process of addition can be separated from the algorithm. The old way to teach addition was to go from right to left adding the ones, then the tens, then the hundreds' place, and so on. By contrast, separating the algorithm from the concrete concept allows your child to apply the problem solving methods of divide and conquer and repeated improvement presented in the last chapter.

Thinking of math in terms of problem solving is particularly useful when coming up with estimates in one's head. When doing addition in your head, it is best to go from left to right. For example, when adding 10,324 and 2,617, you first know that it is more than 12,000.

Then you add the next place and know that it is more than 12,900, and so it is about 13,000. If the first number had been 10,624, then after adding 600 plus 600 from the hundreds place, you would go back and know that it was more than 13,200. Also teach your child to break numbers down for multiplication. To multiply 12 by 4, your child can first figure out that it is a little more than $10 \times 4 = 40$. Then, if he or she has time or the need, your child can add $2 \times 4 = 8$ to 40 to get 48. Another way to get approximate answers is to rely on the number 10. To calculate a tip at a restaurant, teach your child to take 10% of the bill and to multiply that by 2 to get 20%. Or, for less stellar service, your child can take 10% of the bill and add to it half of that amount to compute a tip of 15%.

Coming up with estimates can also be beneficial for acquiring a broad understanding of the world. For example, consider the question of estimating how many cars there are in the United States. This can be easily estimated from the population if you make simple assumptions, such as there being one car for every two people. To solve problems like this, your child first needs to know some basic numbers such as the population of the United States, which is about 300 million. This exercise is a great example of a problem leading to new knowledge beyond the original problem. By trying to estimate the number of cars in the United States, your child has learned the population of the United States, either by you telling the child or by the child looking it up, and next time, when your child needs to estimate the number of tacos consumed by Americans every year, your child will be ready.

4.3 Language: Looking into Someone Else's Head

Language binds us together. Just by talking, we can put the concepts and models that are in our heads into other people's heads, creating a shared culture. Our culture is expanded by reading and writing, which enables us to exchange concepts and models with people we have never even met.

Articulate the Point Exactly

Like with articulating models discussed in Chapter 2, encourage your children to be as articulate as possible in speech and writing. You don't need to push highfalutin speech patterns, and it isn't necessary to overly stress proper grammar, but you should encourage your children to say *exactly* what they mean. Saying exactly what they mean forces children to examine their concepts and models and helps feed the curiosity cycle. Communication is also improved because being precise cuts down on ambiguity and lowers the probability that the speaker and the hearer both think they are talking about the same thing when they are not. Encourage exactness in speech in everyday situations around the house. For instance, when your child asks where an object is, say "the third drawer down on the left" instead of simply "over there."

As children learn to articulate what is in their own minds, they also learn to identify their emotional states. We will see in Part II that children need to learn models of their own thinking to mitigate the cognitive biases and emotional reactions that we are prone to as embodied humans.

Foreign Language for Multiple Interpretations

Knowing a little of a foreign language can help make thinking more adaptive by showing your child that ideas can be expressed in multiple ways. One classic example is that in Spanish the adjective comes after the noun, as in *casa blanca*, which literally translates to "house white." Although it sounds funny, if you think about it, it makes just as much sense for the description to come after the thing being described as before. Another example is how you say "I dropped it" in Spanish. It is, *se me cayó*, which translates to "it fell from me." In English, *you* dropped the thing, but in Spanish the blame is pinned conveniently on the object. Knowing that ideas can be said in another way helps to remind your child that knowledge is constructed and that there can be multiple ways to express ideas.

Kids typically do not want to learn a second language unless it is as integrated into their lives as is their first language. But even a little knowledge can go a long way, and there is a multiplicative effect since many languages are similar, such as French and Spanish. Learning even the bare bones of a foreign language opens up little pieces of culture. In English, we use a lot of phrases from foreign languages such as the French *je ne sais quoi*, which means "I don't know what," and is a fancy term used to indicate an indescribable characteristic. For example, you could say that eggs that aren't fried in bacon grease lack a certain *je ne sais quoi*.

Movies are an easy way to get familiar with the sounds of a foreign language and to see what life is like in other countries. Incidentally, old movies are a great way to see what the past was like. To get a real sense of the past, it is better to watch old movies from the past rather than new movies set in the past. For instance, when I saw *North by Northwest*, I was surprised by how many tasks used to require a full-time person doing a job, such as operating elevators. Many of the tasks depicted in the movie are automated or self-service today, and we will see more about job loss due to technology in Part III.

Being Someone Else (For a While)

Stephen King believes that books allow for a telepathy between the author and the reader [55]. Books provide access to another person's web of knowledge, vocabulary, and thought patterns. Taking this even further, a great way to understand a person's experience different from your own is to read a story where that experience is narrated in the first person. For example, to learn what it might be like to be a servant in India, read a book narrated in that way, such as *The White Tiger* by Aravind Adiga.

Books now face increasing competition from other forms of media, but that's okay. Often, video games have detailed stories, or there may be a blog about a topic that your child is interested in. Embrace those sources as well. For reading material, find things to read that challenge your child but aren't so hard that they aren't fun.

To begin the process of reading, teach your child to recognize letter sequences. You can play the pattern game. In the pattern game, you say something like "abxxqv" and see if your child can repeat it back to you. Try to stump each other this way. Also identify the different kinds of words: nouns (things), verbs (actions), adjectives and adverbs (descriptors). Use the simple terms and refer to word types as "things," "actions," and "descriptors." Additionally, write names of objects and put them around the house on note cards. A great book for teaching your children to read is *Teach Your Child to Read in 100 Easy Lessons* [31].

The mechanics of reading and writing is the simple part. The hard part is learning to express complex ideas and understanding the meaning of what is read. Once your children learn to read and write, encourage reading and writing at every opportunity by having them write notes and cards and e-mails to relatives and friends. Encourage your child to write about what he or she finds interesting; it doesn't matter if it doesn't follow a standard letter format. When reading to your child, or when looking at something your child has read, ask questions that help him or her to individuate concepts, to build models, and to test models.

Tips on Getting Started

Here are some tips for encouraging your child to interact with the world through history, mathematics, and language.

- When a big news event happens such as a revolution in a foreign country, watch it on TV with your child. Try to give your child the background. It is okay if you don't know all the answers to what led up to the event yourself, the goal is to generate curiosity and to raise questions that your child can answer later.

- Constantly point out problems that led to new inventions. Tell children about the state of the world before the problem was solved and have them come up with their own solutions. Then give them the solution that the inventors came up with. Don't be overly concerned with names and dates. Just focus on the problem that had to be solved. For example, how did people plow the fields? Explain that they domesticated animals for extra energy. And how did they get water to those crops? Explain that they dug irrigation ditches. And how did they move heavy things such as rocks? Explain that they had to invent carts with wheels.

- Always ask your child "How many?" when they ask for small things such as grapes.

- Play the function game. Come up with a function, such as adding 1 to any number, and have your child give you numbers. For each number, you respond with the function value for that number. Have the child guess what the function is.

- Articulate tasks around you as algorithms. To fill up a glass of water, say that you (1) put the water under the spout; (2) turn the spout on; (3) hold it until the water fills the glass; and (4) turn the spout off. Have your child point out other tasks that can be thought of as algorithms.

- Try to speak at the edge of your own vocabulary. Children are great at inferring the meaning of unfamiliar words, so use as many different words around your child as possible.

- Make as many literature references as you can remember. When your child asks how high school was for you, begin by saying, "It was the best of times, it was the worst of times."[7]

- When you speak to your child, try to be as specific as possible. As discussed in the chapter, say "the third drawer down on the left" instead of simply "over there."

---

[7]Charles Dickens, *A Tale of Two Cities*.

Part II

Children and Their Embodied Selves

In this section of the book, we make a significant pivot to discuss how our children are affected by their embodiment. An entity is embodied if it is implemented in a particular architecture. Flying machines can be embodied as propeller planes, jet planes, helicopters, or blimps. Each of these architectures has advantages and disadvantages, making some actions easy, such as hovering in a helicopter, and some actions hard, such as landing a jet on a short runway.

Our embodiment comes from evolution. Our brains are the evolved solution to the problem of surviving in an infinitely complex environment with a finite amount of brain mass. This mismatch between the size of the problem and the constraints of the solution means that our embodied brains must take shortcuts, which lead to cognitive biases. Complicating the matter further, the environment in which our brains evolved was different from the one we live in today. That environment was much more dangerous, and survival hinged on group cohesion. We still feel the pull of the group deep within our psyche, and while generally positive, this pull means that we can be pressured and persuaded by others in subtle ways that escape our notice. In the modern world, our children must learn to effectively work in groups while simultaneously being able to maintain their sense of individual empowerment.

To understand their own embodiment and to thrive in our society, our children must learn to build models about their own minds and the minds of others. These models allow children to develop soft skills such as communication. As we will see in Part III, both society and the employment landscape are dramatically changing. These kinds of soft skills will be increasingly necessary in this new environment.

Chapter 5

Mental Embodiment

We feel like we control our lives, but we are only aware of a fraction of the processing that goes on in our brains. Sigmund Freud famously described a battle deep within our subconscious for the right to determine our behavior. This battle was between the three hidden forces of the id, the ego, and the superego. The id was our primal instincts for instant gratification, the superego was the constraints of society and our beliefs in how the world should be, and the ego was the force that intermediated between the id and superego [32, 19].

Modern psychology treats the brain as a computational machine by focusing on the problems the brain must solve in order for us to behave effectively in our complex and dangerous environment. These modern computational approaches still stress the role of hidden forces in shaping our behavior, but the hidden forces take the form of computation-saving biases and shortcuts in our thinking. This chapter discusses how to teach our children about the biases of their brains so that they can slow down and think when necessary and avoid the errors associated with blindly following their instincts.

5.1 Limited Computational Capacity

Our brains have limited processing capacity that comes in two forms: fast parallel processing and slow serial processing [48, 49].[1] The slow serial part of our brain is our conscious processing; this is what we use when listening to a conversation. Because it is serial, you will notice that you can't listen to two conversations at the same time. Sometimes it feels like you can, but if you pay attention, you'll notice that what you are actually doing is quickly switching back and forth between the two conversations.

The fast parallel part of our brain is subconscious. This is the part of the brain we use when we recognize faces or think about problems without thinking about them consciously. We've all had the experience of an answer to a question just popping into our heads; this is because the subconscious part of our brain came up with the answer and then tapped on the shoulder of consciousness. Both the serial and the parallel parts of our brains have limited capacity and are therefore scarce resources that your child needs to maximize.

Limited Serial Processing

The conscious, slow serial part of the brain is susceptible to distractions. We can only do one thing at a time,

---

[1]These are rough terms and not entirely accurate because the "slow serial" part of our brain is not really serial, it just feels that way. However, these terms are easy to understand and remember. Kahneman [49] calls the slow serial part of our brain "System 1" and the fast parallel part of our brain "System 2."

and it is hard to switch back and forth. This is why we shouldn't study with the TV on.[2] Every time you switch to something else, like checking what is going on in the TV show you are watching, your serial brain is not working on the problem at hand. Even worse, once you try to switch back to your task, it takes time and effort to bring the details of what you were working on back into short-term memory.

A consequence of our limited serial processing ability is that we can only think of, and place value on, a small number of things at once. This means that different people focus on different things to value at different times. This mismatch of focus is often on hilarious display at homeowners association meetings. Some people are concerned about the flowers at the subdivision entrance. Others worry about cars driving too fast or about liability from the neighborhood pond. Still others worry about how much was spent on the Fourth of July party. These are all pertinent issues, but it's amusing to watch how we tend to focus on one or a few issues and ignore the rest.

One summer, I started to see droppings around the neighborhood, and I became worried that we had rats (fortunately, it turned out they were just toads). I was talking with a neighbor about the situation, and she had no interest in the droppings at all. Instead, she wanted to tell me about the rattlesnake in her yard. It was funny; I knew that in the rock-paper-scissors of household dangers that rattlesnakes beat rodents, but I didn't want to hear about the snake. I was focused on rats.

---

[2]See [89] for a discussion and pointers to relevant literature for why deliberate, concentrated practice is important for good grades.

Limited Parallel Processing

The subconscious, fast parallel part of the brain is also a scarce resource that you want to direct to work on productive tasks. It seems to work on the things that you process with your serial brain. So if you watch television programs, it will work on the story lines. Teach your children to direct this processing power toward productive parts of the curiosity cycle by encouraging them to keep current important problems in their heads. This means consciously revisiting and thinking about questions that are still unanswered. For instance, when trying to come up with examples for this book, I would write down concepts that needed examples and then head home on my commute. Those open questions were processed in the background, and the examples would just pop into my head. Scientists keep the problems they are working on in their heads at all times; that way answers will occur to them at unexpected moments, such as when they are in the shower.

This background processing is an important part of the curiosity cycle. When you individuate a new concept, this provides kindling for your parallel brain because it can work on how this new concept might be put together with other concepts to build new models. New models make further use of our background processing because this processing can continuously scan perceptual input for confirming or contrary evidence to the model.

Even further in the background is the time we spend asleep. During our dreams, we work on consolidating the memories we created during the day by "practicing" during our sleep. In fact, scientists have found that if they put rats through a maze and watch the firing patterns of their brains as they traverse the maze, they can see those same firing patterns while the rats sleep, indicating that they are practicing.[3] I like to think that dreams even allow us to practice situations that we haven't yet experienced. I once dreamed that I lost control of my car and drove it into a lake. I couldn't open the windows or doors, and I said to myself as I was drowning, "Next time, I should roll down the windows before I hit the water."

5.2 Imperfect Memory

We will see in Chapter 8 that the way human memories are organized provides a significant advantage over how computers store information. Chapter 8 will also discuss how computer memory lacks the deep associations with thinking that makes human cognition so robust. In this section, we will focus on how the human method of storing memories also has significant disadvantages, and we will see why your child should be aware of the limitations of our memory and their associated pitfalls.

Fragile and Easily Overwritten

Thinking and memory are intimately connected. Our brain only stores the gist of situations, and our imagination reconstructs the rest based on what makes sense.[4] This is why we are such incompetent eyewitnesses. When we remember something, we don't simply pull a complete memory out of our brain like we pull a sock out of a

---

[3]See the NOVA special *What Are Dreams?* http://www.pbs.org/wgbh/nova/body/what-are-dreams.html.

[4]Gilbert [36] is the reference for this subsection on how memory is fragile and easily overwritten.

drawer—we build the memory from fragments. When we are done with the memory, this reconstructed memory becomes our new memory that is placed back in the sock drawer.

Our memories are thus changed every time we recall them, and the more they are recalled the more they change. At the extreme, I have memories that I no longer remember, but I still have them because I remember remembering them. For many of my earliest childhood memories, I no longer recall the actual event, but I have a memory of recalling it, and that memory now serves as the original. This difference between remembering and remembering remembering is made clear to me when an unusual event, such as coming across an old picture, triggers an actual early childhood memory that I have not thought about in decades.

Limited and Associative

Our memories are limited and associative. In our short-term memory, we can only remember a few things at once (around seven) before we either have to write them down or expend the effort to move them to long-term memory [76]. This is why we need to-do lists. Our memories are also associative. We've all had the experience of walking into a room and forgetting why we came. This is because what stands out in our memory depends on the situation we are in [73]. I generally remember the reason for my trip once I return to the room where I began the journey.

Our web of knowledge and our memories are intertwined. Once while walking in the woods, I asked my uncle about which plants were edible. As we went along the trail, and he came up with plants, he would remember stories from his childhood. His recollection went something like this: "Dandelions, the flowers can be used to make wine. I once picked boxes full for a neighbor; he paid five cents for a large cardboard box. There are cattails and cowslips. For cowslips, Mom had us kids pick the leaves, and she cooked them up like spinach. Queen Anne's lace is the original carrot and ... of course there is Juneberry. Aunt Leona made great Juneberry pie."

External Memory

Our imperfect memory means that you should teach your child to store reminders externally in the environment. To-do lists are great, but we can do more to prepare our environment to minimize the risk of failure. A classic example is not putting your keys in the trunk. If you instead put your keys on the bumper, you don't have to run the risk of forgetting and locking them in the trunk.

A memorable example of not properly preparing the environment comes from the first DARPA Grand Challenge in 2004.[5] The Grand Challenge was a 150-mile long autonomous robot race. The race took place in the desert in the western United States and was sponsored by the Defense Advanced Research Projects Agency (DARPA). One of the teams in the race had an autonomous motorcycle. Anthony Levandowski worked on this autonomous motorcycle for six months. When the moment of starting the race finally arrived, Anthony forgot to switch on the stability control, and the bike immediately fell over and was disqualified. Six months of work went down the drain because he forgot to flip a switch. A colleague of

---

[5]See *The Great Robot Race* Nova video for an introduction to the DARPA Grand Challenge.

mine[6] noted that the real mistake was not forgetting to flip a switch. The real mistake occurred well before that, in designing the system in such a way that forgetting to flip a switch could so easily end in failure.

The importance of setting up the environment also applies to safety. If a child is injured in the home, the mistake may not have been taking your eyes off the child for that moment, but rather setting up the environment so the injury could occur. This is why there is so much emphasis now on childproofing the home. For example, when I was two years old, I pulled a TV down off its stand. Luckily, it didn't fall on me. Nowadays, we know that all furniture should be secured. There will always be unfortunate accidents and bad luck, but the probability of bad luck can be lowered through preparation.

5.3   Abundant Patterns

Our brains are amazing at recognizing *patterns*. A pattern is a recurring theme in the environment. Patterns are like concepts because you can individuate them to pull them out of experience, and patterns are also models because they can be used for prediction (although patterns are models that do not contain causal explanations).

Examples of Patterns

Someone's face is a pattern. The interstate highway system is another. Highways with odd, two-digit numbers go north and south, and highways with even two-digit numbers go east and west. Highways with three-digit

---

[6]Joseph Modayil

numbers, beginning with an even number, loop around major cities.

Movies also have patterns in them (too many). Our protagonists come up with a plan, and it looks like it is going to work, but then, suddenly, something goes wrong and our protagonists have to improvise, but it doesn't look like it is going to work. But then, suddenly, there is a miraculous event such as an earlier character having a change of heart and swooping in to save the day, and our protagonists prevail. TV is also ripe with patterns. I found *Law and Order SVU* to be less interesting once I recognized its pattern. The story looks like it is going to unfold one way, but then, at the 15-minute mark, there is a twist, and it looks like the story is going another way. Things look about wrapped up at minute 44, but then at minute 45, there is another plot twist. Of course, the story wraps up by minute 60. (I'm hard on *SVU*, but at least they deviate from the pattern sometimes, unlike, say, *Perry Mason*.) We will see in Part III that recognizing these patterns is hard for computers and is a key reason why computers are so uncreative.

Patterns to Superstitions

Our brains are so tuned to recognize patterns that we often find patterns even where there are none [42]. Superstitious thinking arises because we "learn" patterns that don't exist in nature. Even random processes don't look random to us because our brains tend to find little clusters of events that look significant. Superstitious thinking led "doctors" in the Stone Age to drill holes in people's heads to let out the evil spirits [7]. Closer to modern day, professional baseball players are famous for their superstitions [13]. Superstitions even exist among people who aren't professional athletes. When I was a kid, it was common for a person to carry around a severed foot of a rabbit for "good luck." Clearly, it didn't do the rabbit much good, but someone must have at some point seen a pattern between a rabbit's foot and some fortunate events.

The curiosity cycle can help your child minimize superstitious thinking. For example, sometimes when you read your horoscope, it sounds like it perfectly applies. But, if your child uses the curiosity cycle to predict the world through models, he or she will realize that there is no causal mechanism for the alignment of the stars, or whatever, to actually have a predictable effect on anyone's life. Using a model helps to weed out coincidences that seem like real patterns.

Your child also needs to realize that we are often too lazy to use the serial part of our brain and instead fall back on pattern matching. To see this, consider the following question: A bat and ball together cost $1.10. The bat costs $1.00 more than the ball. How much does the ball cost? Our instinct is to use pattern matching to come up with an answer of $0.10, but pattern matching leads us astray in this case.[7] Although we can't stop and think about every little thing in our complex world, our children must learn when a situation requires more consideration. To do this, they need to learn to identify clues by monitoring both their own mistakes and the environment. In this case, the clue comes from the environment—if the question were as simple as it appeared, no one would bother to ask it.

---

[7]Taken from Kahneman [49] The bat costs $1.05, and the ball costs $0.05.

5.4 Cognitive Biases

Our brains are biased to see the world in particular ways. Two reasons for these biases are (1) the world is different now than it was when our brains evolved (primitive humans didn't have to make decisions about saving for retirement); and (2) we have limited computational resources and are unable to calculate everything correctly. Children must know about their biases so that they can avoid them and make sound decisions. Children also need to keep in mind that other people suffer from these same biases. This recognition will help children to better predict people's behavior. Learning about biases is also a way to get children interested in how their own brains work.

Biases and Comparisons

Humans have difficulty making absolute value judgments when evaluating options, so we like to compare things relative to each other [2]. We want to make comparisons even when there is nothing obvious to compare to. This desire to make comparisons causes us to rely on reference values (called *anchors*). The classic example of anchoring is having someone guess the population of a country, such as Brazil. If you first ask the person if the population is less than or greater than 50 million, the person's guess of the population will likely be lower than it would be if you had first asked if the population of the country were less than or greater than 200 million. This difference in estimates occurs because the anchor (reference) point in the first case is lower [102].

More practically, anchoring occurs in salary negotiations where the applicant tries to anchor the salary negotiations at a high number, such as what the top person in the field makes, and the interviewer tries to anchor the salary at a lower number, such as the average wage of a bricklayer in Cambodia. Comparisons are also related to how our expectations shape our evaluations of events. You might be annoyed when you have to wait a long time for your food at a restaurant, but some of the sting of the wait can be mitigated by comparing the experience to that of hunting a wild boar with a stick.

One situation in which we do a particularly poor job of making comparisons is when something is "free" [2]. There may occasionally be a free lunch, but often that free lunch comes at the expense of something else. The value of that something else is called the *opportunity cost*. An opportunity cost is the cost of the next best thing that you cannot do because you are doing something else. If you go to the movies from 2:00 p.m. to 4:00 p.m., then you can't garden during that time. So the cost of the movie is the price of admission plus the value of gardening. When things are free, we often forget about the opportunity cost. Explain to your child that if he or she stands in line for an hour to get a free funnel cake, that is an hour lost on the playground. Incidentally, it's funny how opportunity costs are often missing from inspirational quotations on the Internet such as "You miss 100% of shots you don't take." Well, you could try passing the ball.

Something being free can also cost us in other ways besides time. Your child will want to download "free" programs and apps that will ask for personal information or possibly install malware. With friends and family, people give away things all the time, and this is wonderful. But strangers and organizations giving away something for free is another example of when it is important to model other people's models and intentions. When presented with something for free, children should ask themselves, "What do they hope to gain by giving away something for free?"

Biases and Models

Humans have biases in how we create concepts and build models. When it comes to models about ourselves, there is a bias to be overconfident. For example, ninety percent of people think that they drive better than most [102]. Being overconfident may be great for our mental health, but your child needs to be able to identify this bias. Additionally, an interesting bias I've noticed in myself and others is that once we learn a concept or fact, we immediately can't imagine anyone not knowing it.

Confirmation bias is the tendency to notice things that confirm our prior beliefs and discount things that do not [71]. If you believe that Hollywood doesn't make good movies anymore, then every old good movie is going to reinforce that belief and be more salient to you than an old bad movie. The opposite will be true for new movies. *Motivated reasoning* is the tendency to believe in things you want to believe. This was well put by Upton Sinclair: "It is difficult to get a man to understand something when his salary depends upon his not understanding it!" When waterless urinals were introduced a few years back, experts said they were safe and would save water, but plumbers vehemently argued that those toilets were unsanitary and should not be used [24].

Biases and Time

When it comes to kids, the mother of all cognitive biases has to be weighing the future too little, and the next chapter will discuss the alluring power of having the cookie NOW! Another important bias is the over-reliance or focus on recent salient events [50]. Recall that following hurricane Katrina, everyone was focused on hurricanes. Projections were made that were driven by the strong emotional event of Katrina, and they didn't adequately take into account historical data in the tone of their warnings. In the spring of 2011, the focus was on tornadoes.

Another example comes from Super Bowl XXX in 1996 when the Pittsburgh Steelers played the Dallas Cowboys. Larry Brown was a backup cornerback who made two interceptions by being in the right place at the right time. After the season, he was in big demand, and the Oakland Raiders gave him a contract worth $12.5 million. It was a waste of money. He never lived up to the expectations created by that performance. The Raiders paid him too much because they were overly focused on the recent salient event of the Super Bowl.

Tips on Getting Started

Here are some tips on helping children learn to be aware of the limitations of their own brains.

- Point out errors in thinking and memory to your children, both the errors that you make and the errors that they make. The tone should not be a critical one but rather one of detached curiosity. For example, if you forget to pick something up while at the store, talk your child through how it may have happened. It could be something like, "We were in the bread isle on our way to the bagels, but then you brought up Star Wars and we walked on autopilot right past them."

- A fun way to explore the biases of the human brain with your child is to get a book of optical illusions. The illusions illustrate to your child that the world is not always as it appears.

- Ask children why they performed certain actions, and ask what they were thinking at the time. The idea is to get them to examine their own thought processes.

- To give your child a sense of how ephemeral some things are that we consider important, point out hot topics in the news and in conversations surrounding your child. Even better, point out topics that were important a few months ago but are no longer mentioned. It could be something like, "Remember how two months ago we were all worried about ..."

Chapter 6

Physiological Embodiment

The last chapter discussed the brain as a computational machine, and in this chapter, we turn our attention to the interaction between the brain and the body. This interaction is important because it allows us to comprehend abstract concepts such as love and time through metaphors to bodily experience [60]. This understanding through metaphors is possible because we live in physical bodies that allow us to directly interact with physical objects. For example, the concept of "a theory" can be understood through a metaphor to a building. The theory can have a strong or a weak *foundation*. If it is incomplete, it is just a *framework*. A theory can also need more *support* so that it doesn't *collapse*.

In last chapter's focus on computation, we also neglected the role of emotions in decision making. Your child has to be aware that emotions can alter how he or she appreciates a situation. The more your child is aware of the power of emotions, the more likely it is that he or she can avoid their pitfalls. We will also see in this chapter that being aware of the natural tendencies of the mind can enable children to rise above living on autopilot so that they can access their inner philosopher.

6.1 Metaphors: From the Physical to the Abstract

Your child's web of knowledge grounds out in physical experience. All that time spent playing with blocks and dumping over milk enables your child to later understand abstract concepts through metaphors to that physical experience

Recognizing that we see the world through metaphors helps children have adaptive thinking because it reminds them that the world must be interpreted, and therefore that knowledge is fluid and tentative. Being mindful of metaphors also helps with communication because realizing that someone can comprehend a situation using a different metaphor can help your child understand that person more easily.

Metaphors Help Us Understand the Abstract

There are multiple examples of how metaphors help us understand abstract concepts.[1] One example is that feelings are mapped to "up" and "down," where happiness is "up" and sad is "down." You can tell someone to *cheer up*, and you can tell when someone is feeling *low*. Another

---

[1]Much of this discussion is based on the work of Johnson and Lakoff [60, 45].

example is that time is a scarce resource, like money. For instance, you might observe that you *wasted* two hours at the DMV.

Metaphors determine how we think about ideas. There is a common metaphor that an argument is a war, and you could say something like "she attacked my argument," but as we will see in Chapter 7, it is more productive to think about an argument as a cooperative job. Another famous example is the metaphor "love is war." You hope for a relationship characterized, not by war, but by something more productive like a journey. In the "love is a journey" metaphor, it is a long, cooperative affair with a beginning, a middle, and an end. (Okay, so the "end" part isn't so positive.)

Metaphors are so deeply ingrained in our language that we often don't even think about them. We say things like "don't count your chickens before they hatch" or "kill two birds with one stone." For the latter, the underlying metaphor pops out if you replace "stone" with "rock." Killing birds just sounds cruel, although, admittedly, not as cruel as skinning a cat. Why on earth would anyone do that?

Physical Experience is the Foundation of Knowledge

Physical experience in the world is the foundation for your child's web of knowledge, and his or her physical experience can be augmented with basic activities around the house. As mentioned previously, you can provide non-traditional toys such as a spring, a tape measure, and a scale. Your children can get a lab notebook and write down how much different things weigh. They can put water in a cup and set it outside to see how much evaporates, or on a cold day, how long it takes to freeze. They can test friction on different surfaces by rubbing objects over wax paper and linoleum, and you can explain that lack of friction is why wet linoleum or tile is dangerous. Your child can observe that when a glass of water is just barely too full, the water still holds together.

Try to come up with physical, concrete ways to show your child the world. Pour the same amount of water into different-sized glasses and show that the total value does not change even though the water is higher in a tall, skinny glass than it is in a short, fat glass. Demonstrate day and night on a basketball with a flashlight standing in for the sun. Explore the five senses by doing traditional activities such as having them close their eyes and identify from which direction a sound came.

The link between abstract knowledge and physical experience underscores the need for unstructured play. Children should get out and see nature. They can observe how a lily pad floats on water, and they can do a belly flop in the pool and know it hurts.

Analogies: Transferring Knowledge

Like a metaphor, an analogy is a way to use what one knows about one concept to understand another. In an analogy, if a familiar concept has properties A, B, and C, and we can show that a less-familiar concept has properties A and B, then we can infer that the less-familiar concept probably also has property C. You can teach your child to use analogies in everyday conversation.

Analogies are particularly valuable for model building. Encourage your children to find instances of learned models in completely different areas. For example, if you teach your children to play chess, they may learn about the coordinate system on the board. Starting on the white side on the left with $A1$, the coordinate system uses a number and a letter to mark each square of the board. Then, when you want to teach a child about a math coordinate system, you can use chess as an analogy. In general, encourage your children to always be making connections. It's great when they say things such as "Oh, it's like ..."

Analogies often show up on tests for intelligence or giftedness,[2] although they often seem to be evaluating whether your child can determine what properties two concepts have in common. One example is "chicken is to egg as cow is to x." The answer for x is "milk," and the property they both have in common is *produces*. Another example is "wheel is to circle as window is to x." In this case, an answer for x is "rectangle" and the property that carries over is *shape*. Try to stump your kids with these kinds of analogy questions to get them thinking this way.

Analogies are also needed for creativity.[3] As we saw in Chapter 5, humans are really good at pattern matching, and this allows us to reason by analogy and to make the kind of leaps of understanding that are essential for creativity. In Part III, we will see how the inferior pattern matching capability of computers is one of the reasons why they are not nearly as creative as toddlers.

---

[2]For example, see Johnson and Corn [46]

[3]Hawkins [41] makes a good argument that analogies are important for creativity.

6.2   Emotions: Taming Ancient Passions

Thinking with emotions confers an evolutionary advantage because if our ancestors didn't get mad and lash out when someone took their piece of the kill, people would have taken from them all of the time, and we wouldn't be here. But in the modern world, with the rule of law, emotions can get us into complicated situations. Your child needs to understand his or her own emotions and model the emotions of others.

Emotions are Judgments

Emotions are intelligent because they involve evaluations (judgments) of situations [96]. For instance, at some level, we *decide* that what someone did was wrong, and that's what makes us angry. Realizing that emotions involve judgments can give us power over them. For example, if it is best not to get angry, we can try to revise our judgment of the situation by emphasizing the other person's perspective.

Mental States Influence Behavior

Your child should be aware of *hot states* and *cold states*. Hot states occur when we are viscerally charged either by a drive, such as hunger, or an emotion. Cold states occur when we are our cool, rational selves [68]. When we are in a hot state, we may make decisions that would differ from the decisions we would make in a cold state, such as succumbing to the smell of baked cookies. On top of this, we do a poor job of predicting how we will act in hot states [2]. Teach your child to identify when he or she is in a hot state and to account for how thinking changes in hot states.

Hot and cold states are linked to temptation. In a cold state, you may decide that you shouldn't eat any donuts that day, but if they are put in front of you, your state may warm up a bit. I once told my oldest son (age six at the time) that he couldn't have any more donuts from the box sitting on the kitchen table. He stared at the box and asked in a pained voice, "Daddy, please close the box." I closed the box, but he was still visibly distressed. He then said, "Oh, Daddy, that's not enough, please put the box away." There is a classic experiment in which a young child is left alone in a room with a cookie (or some other treat). The experimenter says that if the child can wait and not eat the cookie, an even better treat will be offered when the experimenter returns in a few minutes [77]. We can imagine that waiting would be difficult, and it has been found that children's ability to exhibit self-control early in life leads to more success later in life [79].

Fear Is the Mind-Killer

> *I must not fear. Fear is the mind-killer. Fear is the little-death that brings total obliteration. I will face my fear. I will permit it to pass over me and through me. And when it has gone past I will turn the inner eye to see its path. Where the fear has gone there will be nothing. Only I will remain.*
>
> — Frank Herbert, *Dune*

Resisting temptation points to the larger truth that while emotions are judgments, they don't have to determine our actions. Fear is one emotion that often has a detrimental effect on our behavior. My son (age 8 at the time) was once preparing to speak in front of his whole school of 500 people. It was pointless to try to convince him not to be scared—I instead focused on convincing him to do what he needed to do regardless of his fear.

On the subject of fear, one old trick worth mentioning is that since looking someone in the eye is seen as a sign of confidence, tell your child to make a habit of noticing the color of people's eyes. Making eye contact will make your child appear more confident.

6.3   Toward Our Inner Philosopher

Being self-aware in terms of emotions and cognitive biases helps children move beyond their inner animal toward their inner philosopher. A philosopher is a person who stops and thinks [17]. Thinking does more than enable children to tame the passions of their emotions and avoid the pitfalls of acting solely on instinct—thinking helps children see the world as it really is.

We Take the Lazy Route

Our finite brains try to avoid unnecessary computation. As a result, we tend to follow the path of cognitive ease, and we prefer to believe in ideas that don't tax us too much or are familiar or easy to understand [49]. Just like with the example of old Hollywood movies and the confirmation bias from Chapter 5, we try to prove our ideas by looking for examples that confirm our beliefs, instead of trying to disprove them the way that scientists do.

Teach your children to question their ideas and beliefs. Questioning leads to model refinements and helps to spin the curiosity cycle. Paradoxically, a consequence of the curiosity cycle is that as we learn more, we become less sure of our knowledge. This is wonderful. To fully appreciate how beautiful doubt can be, consider the opposite as embodied in the combination of ignorance and certainty that accompanies the comments section of Internet news articles.

We Seek Cohesion

Our brains want the world to be simple and orderly, so we sacrifice truth for coherence [49]. Hollywood provides us with movie characters that are either all good or all bad, even though most people are a combination of both and our behavior is heavily influenced by our environment. Both trusted news organizations such as the New York Times and news organizations that are trusted less evenly such as Fox News are often guilty of presenting simplified narratives. They are rooting for different sides, but they both take one-sided positions and present them as truth.

Teach your children that the world is not as simple as their minds want it to be, and teach them to not let what they want to be true influence what they believe to be true. In addition, teach your children to consider the sources of information. Paying attention to the sources of information is especially important on the Internet where respected organizations such as BBC News have to compete with obscure ones. Our children should understand that not all news stories on Google News are equally credible.

Our desire for an orderly world also causes us to overlook the importance of luck [49]. We saw in Chapter 5 that our brains look for patterns, even when there are none, and so we make up explanations for random events. For example, I love it when sports announcers proclaim that some teams just "find a way to win." Imagine a tournament like the "March Madness" college basketball tournament that begins with 64 teams. Our tournament is unique in that each team is represented as a coin. When two coins "play" each other, they are flipped together until one coin comes up heads and the other tails, and the coin that comes up heads wins. After the first round, there would be 32 teams left, then 16, then 4, then 2, and finally a winner. Sports announcers watching this tournament would certainly declare that the winning coin, a plucky 1973 quarter, just knows how to fight through adversity and "finds a way to win." That quarter really came to play. I give credit to the coaching.

We Fail to Recognize Tradeoffs

My favorite example of our brains running on autopilot is our inability to recognize tradeoffs. The idea of tradeoffs was introduced in Chapter 5 in the discussion of "opportunity costs." Tradeoffs seem simple, but we humans are surprisingly bad at recognizing them. As an example, consider the width of streets in a housing subdivision. Once the houses are built, the wider you make the streets, the less front yard the houses will have. In a neighborhood near my own, emergency vehicles had trouble navigating the narrow streets. When asked what should be done, people thought that the streets should be widened.

But when it was pointed out that widening the streets would reduce yard space, that idea lost its appeal.

A consequence of our failure to recognize tradeoffs is that the answer we are likely to give to a question is partially determined by how that question is asked. Should the streets be widened to accommodate emergency vehicles? Of course. Should my yard be shortened to accommodate emergency vehicles? Get off my property.

Tips on Getting Started

Here I provide some tips on helping children see the world through metaphors and emotions and helping them move toward their inner philosopher.

- Knowing that we see the world through metaphors helps your child with adaptive thinking because it gives him or her a sense that something can be understood using more than one metaphor. Try to look for multiple metaphors to represent ideas in your everyday environment. For example, marketers have recently changed the metaphor of having a pet from being a "pet owner" to being a "pet parent." Talk about how changes in metaphors change how you view a situation and ultimately how you behave. Do your kids think that a "parent" would be more caring than an "owner" and would therefore spend more money on pet supplies?
- Point out tradeoffs in the environment. For example, you could say, "If you don't accompany me to the grocery store, you will lose the opportunity to lobby for your favorite foods."

- Point out emotional states in both you and your children. Say something like, "Earlier, when you were angry, you wanted to x, but now that idea doesn't seem so appealing." For example, you could tell them how you were once angry with the insurance company for raising their rates, but when you calmed down, you felt that switching would be too much trouble. In this case, neither feeling is more right than the other, but what is interesting and worth teaching your child is the change in perspective you experienced as you transitioned from the hot state of being angry to the cold state of normalcy.
- Remind the child to "stop and think" when he or she jumps to a conclusion.
- Part of being a philosopher is overcoming emotions when necessary. Instead of trying to convince a child not to be scared, convince the child to do what needs to be done despite being scared.

Chapter 7

Social Embodiment

In addition to living within the confines of our mental and physiological embodiment, we are socially embodied in our surrounding culture. As we saw in Chapter 3, human culture has given rise to profound achievements such as radios and air travel. These grand achievements are possible even though each of us individually only possesses a small amount of specialized knowledge. I often think about how worthless I would be if you sent me back in time 10,000 years. I could describe technologies, but I wouldn't be able to help them build any of it. We are able to achieve so much because we can pool our knowledge and work together.

Working together requires being able to deduce how others perceive a situation and what their intentions are, and it also requires the ability to communicate our own perceptions and goals. Understanding other people can be challenging because we can't directly see into their minds. We can only get hints of what they are thinking from their choice of words, tone of voice, physical gestures, and facial expressions. We are remarkably good at processing these clues, but they are only clues. This chapter discusses how to use shared experience and models of other people's minds to understand others and thrive in social environments.

7.1 Theory of Mind

Around the age of four, children begin to develop a theory of mind [8]. They start to reflect on their own thinking, and they begin to understand that other people can hold beliefs that are different from reality. For example, imagine that a child sees an adult put a penny in a box, and imagine that the child later sees someone else remove the penny while the adult is not looking. Children under the age of four will generally think that the adult thinks that the penny is no longer in the box—they can't separate what the adult knows from what they know. Older children can recognize that the adult has a belief that is different from reality and different from their own.[1] This kind of understanding is the beginning of making models of other people's models, and in addition to being necessary for communication, such models are particularly important for outsmarting others and keeping from falling prey to scams and frauds.

Game Theory

Game theory is an academic area that focuses on understanding competition between people. A critical component of game theory is modeling your opponent. Sports

---

[1]See the interesting video http://www.pbs.org/wnet/humanspa rk/episodes/program-three-brain-matters/video-full-episo de/418/.

provides many great examples. In soccer, certain types of fouls give the other team a penalty kick from close range. The only chance a goalie has to save a penalty kick is to (1) correctly guess whether the kicker is going to aim the ball at the left or right side of the goal; and (2) dive that way. As a soccer goalie, I was taught to look at the hips of the kicker to get information about which way the ball is going to go. This was a useful model and allowed me to stop many kicks. But later in life, when I was no longer a goalie and was taking penalty kicks, I realized that I could exploit my knowledge that goalies have this model. I taught myself to point my hips in one direction and kick the ball in the other direction. This was quite successful because goalies used their model and watched my hips and dove to the wrong side.

Another example of the benefits of modeling other people's models comes from baseball. In Little League Baseball, it was once conventional wisdom that a batter should never swing at the first pitch. The thinking was that if the first pitch was a ball, then the batter would be ahead in the count and have an advantage. The result of this norm was that the first pitch was generally a fastball right down the middle. On top of the predictability of the location and type of the first pitch, the defense generally was not expecting anything to happen on that pitch. This situation could be exploited by aggressively hitting the first pitch. Of course, this type of out-thinking the opponent only works until the other side catches on, but by then your child can be exploiting the next set of models.

Selling and Fraud

Advertisers and fraudsters are trying to hack your child's brain, and models of other people's models are your child's best defense. When your children watch TV with commercials, encourage them to look at the commercials from the sellers' point of view. Teach your child to identify what is being advertised and what methods are being used to make the product look appealing, such as quick frame shots, upbeat music, and scenes of kids having fun. On a related note, it can be enlightening to watch TV with the sound off. See how much you can understand from the situation and the facial expressions—it is surprising how different things look.

Your child will spend a lot of time on the Internet, so this skill of identifying when someone is trying to trick your child is particularly important. For example, scams where people impersonate someone or some company you know via email in order to get your personal information, called phishing scams, are ubiquitous [22]. Your children will likely be targeted for such scams and all other sorts of online mischief. It is useful to teach children about particular tricks, but the kinds of tricks are always evolving, and therefore it is more effective to teach children to build models that can help them determine someone's true intentions. To teach this skill, show your child the online offers that you get and discuss them. When a gentleman from Nigeria sends you an e-mail about making a large sum of money by helping him move a fortune out of the country, show it to your child. See what your child thinks. Try to let your child form an independent opinion before you give yours.

Closer to home, the next time a commercial comes on

TV showing something spectacular that can be yours for three easy payments of only $19.95 (plus shipping and handling), talk about it with your child. Point out that the big $19.95 is what flashes on the screen and that our brains map that to $19. Explain that it appears that the item costs $19, but in reality it costs almost $70 when the three payments are taken into account and you have paid the $9.95 in shipping and handling (whatever "handling" is). These types of shenanigans are particularly noteworthy because they are a legal form of lying.

You can also show your child that piece of mail from the local auto dealership that says your current car is in especially high demand. Teach your child to use his or her models of sellers to determine that what the advertiser is really trying to do is sell cars, and that when you trade in your car, you buy another one. Also teach your child to identify when marketers try to use our curiosity against us. Together, watch one of those online commercials that shows a video clip to try to raise your interest in a story and then directs you to a website to find out which person the zombie ate. If all goes well, your child's response to this kind of thing will be, "How dumb do you think I am?"

7.2 Communication

The goal of communication is shared understanding, and recognizing that knowledge is constructed through concepts and models can help children reach these understandings with others. Recognizing how knowledge is constructed can help children identify communication gaps because it highlights the possibility that other people might construct knowledge differently. Seeing knowledge at the finer level of detail of concepts and models can also help children recognize the possibility that the person they are speaking with may not have a particular concept or model, or that *they* may lack a concept or model.

Relying on concepts and models for communication requires knowing the concepts and models held by the person with whom you are talking. Luckily, much of our experience is shared, and this leads to shared concepts and models. Encourage children to consider the experiences of the person with whom they are talking, because when your child explains an idea to someone, it must be explained relative to what the listener already knows. Your child should get in the habit of making analogies and links to those concepts and models in the listener's current web of knowledge.

Understanding through Shared Physical Experience

We saw in the last chapter that we understand abstract concepts through metaphors to physical experience. One interesting aspect of this physical experience is that it is more or less the same from person to person. We are all about the same size, we have the same kinds of muscles, and we have a similar brain structure. This similarity in the structure of our bodies allows for communication. When you say that an object is heavy, your child knows what you mean because your child has lifted heavy things. The same is true for being sleepy or hungry, or anything else related to bodily feeling. Your child knows what you mean because he or she maps the words you say to his or her own bodily experience.

This similarity of physical experience is particularly important in recognizing emotions; children understand what anger is because they have been angry before. To teach children to recognize the emotions of others, have them pay attention to facial expressions to read those emotions. As mentioned earlier, one way to do this is by watching movies or TV with the sound off and having your child look at the faces and identify the emotions. Here again, you can also watch movies in foreign languages. For example, show a famous French movie without showing the subtitles and see if your child can figure out what is going on just by how the words are spoken. Of course, it may be tough to get a young child to sit through a whole movie in a foreign language, but you can also limit the viewing to particularly interesting scenes.

Showing movies in a foreign language also provides the benefit of giving children a sense of what it is like to not completely understand. As discussed in Chapter 2 and Chapter 3, being comfortable in areas and situations you don't completely understand is an important skill in curiosity-based learning.

Improvisation: Thinking on Their Little Feet

Face-to-face social interaction happens quickly. The pace is much more rapid than interacting with a computer, or just about anything else. You can build this skill with your child. One way to do this is to play the questions-only game. In this game, you may only ask questions. You ask your child a question, and your child must respond with a question. If one player cannot respond with a question, the other player wins. The response question must make sense given the current conversation, it can't repeat a previous question, and it can't be something overly simple such as, "What do you think?"[2] For example, you could ask your child, "Do you like apples?" The child could respond, "Have you ever met anyone who doesn't?" Then, you could say, "Do you really believe that every single person in the world likes apples?" And this sequence of questions continues until someone can't think of a response question in a reasonable amount of time.

You can also practice improvisational comedy with your kids. According to Blanke [11], there are three fundamental principles for improvisational comedy: (1) say "Yes, and ..."; (2) go with your gut; and (3) make everyone else look good. When someone says something, your child can always say, "Yes, and" and fill the rest in with whatever the child wants. For example, you could say, "I rode into camp on a mule." Your child could respond, "Yes, and you told me about all of the gold you found." Improvisation continues from there. This type of technique helps keep conversations going. In conversations, light ones anyway, there usually isn't time for deep thought, so you have to just go with your gut. And for obvious reasons, making everyone else look good is important in both social and professional situations. Get your kids started on making others look good by making sure that they give siblings and friends credit for good ideas.

---

[2]The questions-only game was explained to me by Joseph Mellman.

Arguing to Agree

Arguing isn't about being right; it is a cooperative process whereby two or more people work to come to an agreement about something [110]. If you just want to prove that you are right, and you don't care about the truth, you are not arguing. You are doing something else. Teach your kids to argue with the goal of coming to an agreement by emphasizing that they should focus on figuring out the truth. Watch your child fight with siblings or friends and intercede (but not too much) and steer them toward coming to a new understanding instead of just being right. They, of course, won't immediately dismiss ego and take up the cause of truth, but you can plant the seed. Toward this end, make sure to praise your child if he or she rightfully concedes an argument. In addition, teach your child that a useful subgoal in an argument is to determine where *exactly* the participants do not agree. Often, this technique will clear up misunderstandings, and at the very least it will keep the argument focused.

Losing an argument isn't a bad thing because it means you have learned something. It's funny how in order to learn something you have to admit you were wrong. As part of the curiosity cycle, you always want to be learning and changing. Although, admittedly, learning can be bittersweet sometimes—or just bitter.

Arguing effectively also requires understanding concepts tied to the discussion on logic presented in Chapter 4. For example, teach your child the difference between *necessary* and *sufficient*. Something is necessary if it has to be true in order for something else to be true. To be a car, it is necessary for it to have an engine. Something is sufficient if it alone is enough for something else to be true. It is not sufficient to have an engine to be called a car because a tractor has an engine, but it is not a car. It is sufficient for a car's engine to break for the car to need to be repaired. By contrast, it is not necessary for a car's engine to break for a car to need repairs because the transmission breaking could also cause the car to need repair.

There are two kinds of logical models: inductive models and deductive models. An *inductive model* is a generalization from experience. An example of an inductive model is "American families who live in the suburbs have at least one vehicle." This model isn't always going to be correct, but it can be a useful generalization in some situations. The other kind of model is a *deductive model*, and by the rules of logic it must always be true. For example, if we know that Bob is older than Mary, and Mary is older than Aniket, then we know that Bob is older than Aniket. This type of model must always be true, and a single counterexample proves it to be false.

Searching for counterexamples is an effective way to focus thinking. We saw in the previous paragraph that a single counterexample can disprove a deductive model. Counterexamples can also help articulate inductive models, and by the same process of testing models in the curiosity cycle, counterexamples can lead to new concepts and better models. However, make sure to emphasize to your child that a single counterexample is not sufficient to disprove an inductive model. I remember as a kid I always found it annoying when I proposed an inductive model (okay, half-baked idea), and someone would come up with a single counterexample and think that was the end of it. Counterexamples to an inductive model do not invalidate the model—they offer an opportunity to make it better.

Getting to the truth through logic is essential, but sometimes your child will also need to influence others. In the closing remarks of the second debate before the 1980 election, Ronald Reagan famously asked the audience the rhetorical question, "Are you better off now than you were four years ago?" The late 1970s were a rough time in the US economically, and by asking that question, Ronald Reagan made all of those economic woes salient, and he *framed* the debate in terms of the president's power over the economy. Once framed this way, Jimmy Carter didn't have a chance. Framing is about which aspects of a situation are made to seem important [81]. Our limited brains can't consider everything at once, so your child can change the direction of the spotlight in a way that gives him or her an advantage. Framing is like choosing a metaphor, as described in Chapter 6. We can view love as either a war or a journey, and the metaphor we choose determines which aspects are highlighted in our minds.

Your child can use framing to combat bullying and teasing. Growing up, I was amazed at the ability of some kids to make whatever they were strong on seem important and to make whatever they were weak on seem insignificant. My son was once at school and somebody commented that his hair was too long. This person was highlighting that my son needed a haircut. Had my son been better prepared to frame his response, he might have made it seem like longer hair was a good thing by responding that he liked his hair a little long. As another example, I once saw a child make fun of another child because the second child had never played video games.

The first child was highlighting the lack of experience of the second child. The second child should have retorted that he had better things to do. This response would have raised the profile of a different idea we value, that of doing worthwhile things with our time.

Making Jokes and Telling Stories

Our shared web of knowledge is what makes humor possible. Something is funny when it is not what is expected but nevertheless makes sense because it still follows some known pattern. For example, at the circus we may see a scene where a man in a dog suit walks up to a fire hydrant, and the fire hydrant runs away. This is funny because what we expect to unfold is for the dog to relieve himself on the hydrant, but we are surprised to see the hydrant run away. However, the initially surprising pattern makes sense—if someone were about to pee on you, you would run away too. This recognition is what seems to make us laugh.

Surprise is also important in stories. Stories are a way for us to share experience and bond, and you can help your child learn to tell compelling stories. Your child can learn to tell the story so that by the time the listener gets to the details, the listener cares about them. This is where surprise comes in; knowing the listener's models, the teller can express the story so that there is suspense and surprise.

7.3 Group Dynamics

Acceptance of Authority

Our brains evolved at a time when being excluded from the group meant death. One result of this evolution is that we are wired to trust authority. Stanley Milgram performed experiments in the 1960's at Yale University where he showed that ordinary citizens would inflict pain on innocent people if told to do so by an authority figure [74]. He brought subjects in and told them that they would be taking part in an experiment on memory and learning. He instructed the subjects to give the learner an electric shock every time the learner made a mistake. (There was no actual shock, and the "learner" was in on the experiment and was just play acting.) As the experiment progressed and the subjects were told to administer increasing levels of electric shock, the subjects would become visibly distressed and would ask the experimenter if they could stop. In response, the experimenter would say, "Please continue." The subjects did. More than 60% of the subjects were fully obedient, even when they heard the learner yell out in pain [7].

Even when we are not under the direction of an authority figure, we often treat others poorly when we have too much power. In a mock prison experiment at Stanford University, students were arbitrarily chosen to be either guards or prisoners. Although violence was not allowed in the experiment, the guards became verbally aggressive to the prisoners (remember, these "prisoners" were just random Stanford students just like the guards). The experiment was terminated prematurely after only six days, and while the prisoners were delighted, most of the guards were distressed by the decision to stop the experiment because, presumably, they enjoyed their power and did not want to lose it [39].

Cohesion into Groups

We are social beings, and we are strongly biased to think like those around us [3]. Fashion is a perfect example. Something that was cool last year and could raise someone's status is not cool this year. Another example is a sudden fascination with a particular topic, such as cigars or celebrity chefs.[3] This is the peer pressure that we always talk about, and we even feel this immense pressure to conform as adults. Serious publications such as the *New York Times* print articles that essentially say, "Here is what the cool kids are doing now."[4] The curiosity cycle focuses on teaching children to think for themselves, which should help mitigate the power of peer pressure.

Beyond the pressure to conform, another bias that your child should be aware of is called *group polarization* [80]. Group polarization is the tendency of the members of a close group to take on extreme views because those views are encouraged by the group. Cults come to mind when one thinks about the development of extreme beliefs among members. When a group has a particular viewpoint, individual members can increase their status

---

[3]In the late 1970s and early 1980s truck driving was the career that made a splash on popular culture. There was a TV show called *B. J. and the Bear* where a guy drove around in his truck with his pet chimpanzee, and there were movies like *Smokey and the Bandit* where trucking played a prominent role. The theme came back in the form of "trucker hats" in the early 2000s.

[4]A couple of examples of reporting on what the cool kids are doing now are http://www.nytimes.com/2011/01/16/magazine/16f ob-wwln-t.html and http://www.nytimes.com/2011/07/06/dining /a-bid-to-restore-the-allure-of-the-soda-fountain.html.

by exhibiting this viewpoint, and this creates an arms race to move the views of individual members in an increasingly extreme direction.

We all want and need to be part of a group, but teach your children to be aware of the dangers of group cohesion by emphasizing that they should think for themselves using their own concepts and models.

Tips

Here I provide some tips in helping your child maximize his or her societal embodiment.

- Encourage your child to keep in mind what other people know. For example, when your child talks to Grandma, you could say, "Did Grandma know you had a baseball game today?" This will help with communication and make your child a better story teller. Encourage your child to guess what other people might be thinking.
- Show your children the spam email you get. Talk about the different ways the sender may be trying to trick you. This also applies to the junk mail you receive announcing that you have won various spectacular prizes.
- When watching television, talk about the commercials. Have your child identify the methods that the advertisers are using to make the items look appealing.
- During an argument, teach your kids to identify where exactly the participants do not agree.
- Point out when you see opinions being unjustifiably swayed by the group. If your children say that all

of their friends think team A is swell and team B is bad, point out that there are other groups, equally smart, who think that team B is peachy and team A is an affront to nature.

Part III

Your Child's Future

Part I provided a framework for thinking about how children construct knowledge. Part II described how our thinking is embodied in our brains, body, and culture. It explained how the structure of our brains dictates our computational strengths and weaknesses and how the interaction between our brains and our bodies forms the foundation of our individual knowledge, and it also described how our individual knowledge is shaped by the ideas, communications, and biases of society. In this final Part III, we see how our society will be transformed by technology.

The future belongs to computation, and it will be as alien to us as the present would seem to someone from the Stone Age. Computers are getting smarter, and they are blending our physical and virtual worlds so that we are becoming cyborgs living in augmented reality. Even in the familiar physical reality, robots are popping up everywhere. They don't look like Rosie, the maid from *The Jetsons*. Instead, they are specialized machines that are increasingly becoming embedded in our lives.

We must prepare out children for this future. Most people reading this book were brought into the digital age gradually as new technologies became available, but our children won't have the benefit of this protracted assimilation. They will grow up in a digital world that tracks their every move. While the digital age is now fully here, the ongoing structural revolution in the employment landscape is still unfolding. As they get smarter, computers and robots are displacing human workers, and unlike in the industrial revolution, this new technology does not seem to be creating as many jobs as it destroys. Fortunately, curiosity can prepare our children to thrive in this new world.

Chapter 8

How Computers Think

The continuous advancement of technology means that understanding how computers think will be necessary to be a literate member of society. Computers think using the language of mathematics described in Chapter 4, which includes algorithms, logic, and probability. Algorithms allow computers to do anything that can be precisely written down. Many of these algorithms are used to encode logical operations, and logic was the focus of much of the early research on how to make computers smart. For example, if a computer knows that I am a man, and if it also knows that all men like tacos, the computer can infer that I like tacos. Since the world is often fuzzy, more recent research has focused on reducing common sense to calculation through probability.

A broader way to conceptualize how computers think is as a search over a state space. The idea of a state space is an intimate and implicit part of the curiosity cycle. In Part I, we saw how learning new concepts makes experience richer. When we learn about crown moldings or about different kinds of trees, we see that the world has more possibilities. Imagine that you are standing in a room looking out the window at a tree. After learning about trees and crown moldings, this single state is now one of many possible states:

1. Being in a room *with* crown moldings looking out at a Live Oak.

2. Being in a room *without* crown moldings looking out at a Live Oak.

3. Being in a room *with* crown moldings looking out at a Ceder Elm.

4. Being in a room *without* crown moldings looking at a Ceder Elm.

The set of all possible states is called a *state space*.

Thinking about state spaces provides insight into why computers sometimes seem so dumb and why they can only do *exactly* what you tell them to do. Imagine all of the features that one could notice about a room, such as the color of the walls, the temperature of the air, or whether there is a bottle of ketchup on the floor. The large number of possible features makes for a huge state space, but most of the time, it doesn't matter if there is a crown molding in the room or what kind of tree, if any, is outside the window. We humans are great at ignoring irrelevant information, but computers lack the common-sense knowledge to know which features are relevant in which situation. Ironically, computers' lack of common-sense knowledge causes them to drown in information.

Because they lack commonsense knowledge, computers reason over state spaces using systematic search and systematic memory. Systematic search consists of generating all possibilities and checking to see which ones pan out. When a computer plays chess, it considers all possible moves before choosing one. Actually, the computer does more than that; for each possible move, the computer considers all of the possible moves of its opponent, and then all possible moves for each of these possible moves, and so on. The computer looks as far into the future as time and memory allow.

For humans, knowledge and memories are linked. We do not play chess using systematic search; we only consider promising moves. Systematic search requires a large amount of memory to store all of the possibilities, yet we humans are able to play chess effectively despite our limited memory because of the way our knowledge and memories are structured, as discussed in Chapter 5. In this chapter we will see that, despite computer memory being much more abundant than our own, its usefulness is limited because, just like with features of the world, computers lack the commonsense knowledge that tells them which memories are relevant.

Although computer thought processes are in many ways inferior to our own, there are times when systematic thinking will serve your child well. This chapter will discuss how computers think so that you can teach your child systematic thinking. Children should also know how computers think because, as we will see in the next chapter, they are now doing much of humanity's thinking.

8.1 Systematic Thought

Search

Computers think systematically using search. Systematic search consists of taking how the world is now, figuring out all the ways the world could be, and then determining the kinds of changes that need to be made to get from here to there. A requirement for systematic search is that there be an understanding of all of the ways the world could be. This understanding is called a state space, as we saw earlier. Indeed, a useful way to view a problem or situation is to consider how many possibilities there are. As we saw in Chapter 4, a die has a state space of six states. In chess, the state space is all of the possible locations of the pieces. For a light switch, the state space has two states, "on" and "off." For two light switches, the state space has four states, and for three light switches the state space has eight states $(2 \times 2 \times 2)$.

Consider the example of the Lego minifigure discussed previously, where the arm could be attached in two ways at each end. This gave a state space of four possible ways the arm could be attached. Breaking down a problem makes it easier to solve because the size of the state space is reduced. When applying the forces to put the arm on, the child doesn't have to wonder if it is aligned in the correct way.

Even when the state space is too large to be searched exhaustively, knowing the size of the space can be useful because it helps to think of the environment in terms of the span of possibilities. Consider the set of all possible books that are shorter than 100,000 words.[1] Most of those books would be random combinations of words and look like complete gibberish. Some of those books would be Shakespeare plays. Some books would be better than any known book, others would be ordinary. One of those books would be 100,000 repetitions of the word "cat," and one of those books would be this one. Another one of those books would be this one with the last word changed to "pickle."

Also consider the state space of all possible images. A digital image consists of thousands or millions of *pixels*. Each pixel is a dot of color and is represented in a computer as a combination of the colors red, green, and blue. The value of each of red, green, and blue can be a whole number anywhere from 0 to 255. So the color "red" is represented as $\langle 255, 0, 0 \rangle$, "green" is $\langle 0, 255, 0 \rangle$, and "blue" is $\langle 0, 0, 255 \rangle$. White is $\langle 255, 255, 255 \rangle$, and black is $\langle 0, 0, 0 \rangle$. There are also colors for all possible combinations of those numbers. The "blue" for Facebook is $\langle 59, 89, 152 \rangle$, and the University of Texas at Austin has the official color of burnt orange $\langle 204, 85, 0 \rangle$.

This representation means that there are $256 \times 256 \times 256$ possible colors for each pixel. An iPhone 4 has a camera that takes pictures with five million pixels. This means that there are $(256 \times 256 \times 256)^{5,000,000}$ possible pictures that one could take with an iPhone. This is a huge number, but it is not infinite. Each picture you have ever taken is one of those pictures. This is astounding when you think about it. We see the world as being continuous and infinite, and when we take a picture of

---

[1]Kelly [52] provides an excellent discussion of the Argentinian author Jorge Luis Borges' idea of a library that contains all possible books.

a small part of the world it still seems infinitely large. But with your digital camera, there are a finite number of images that you can take, and each of those possible images is a discrete member of this huge set.

The idea of a state space is intimately tied to the curiosity cycle because we each create our own state space by individuating concepts. When I learned the concept of crown molding, the state-space of a room became larger because in addition to the color of the walls and the type of flooring, each room now either had a crown molding or it did not. Computers are largely incapable of individuating new high-level concepts—they need us to do that for them. But computers can do remarkable things once some part of the world is broken up into discrete pieces, as we will see in the next chapter.

Search is a systematic exploration of all the states to find the one that is best by some measure, and this exploration is done through *actions*. Every move in chess is an action, and picking up a block is an action. Actions are not only necessary to change the world, they are an important part of self-motivated learning [84]. When your child picks up a block, the world has changed, and the options available to your child have changed, and actions that were not possible previously may now be possible. Once your child has picked up the block, he or she can throw it.

In the example of chess, if the computer can evaluate how useful each state is, it can choose the move (action) that is likely to lead it to a good state. Sometimes you won't know how beneficial a state is until you get there, or you won't know what state you will move to until you perform the action. Other times you can simulate the transitions in your mind like a computer does with chess.

The computer thinks, "If I do this, the opponent will do that, then I can do this," and so on, until memory or time is exhausted. This kind of simulation can be useful for your child, as we will see in the next section.

Teaching Search

Your child can use systematic search at school and at play. Consider a word search puzzle. Instead of using a haphazard strategy when looking for a particular word, your child can go row by row checking each letter in each row, and for every letter that matches the first letter, he or she can check those letters around it. If a match for the second letter is found, your child can see if the third letter in the line also matches. If the sequence of letters matches the sought-for word, then it is found. Otherwise, the search continues.

Consider the task of putting together a jigsaw puzzle. For each piece, your child has to figure out the other pieces it is connected to. As your child builds the puzzle, this will get easier and easier because there will be progressively fewer choices. Reducing the number of choices is the principle behind the strategy of starting with connecting the edge pieces. An edge piece usually only connects on three sides instead of four, and two of those connections are always to other edge pieces. These restrictions help to reduce search.

Another example is the puzzle game Sudoku. Here, the goal is to fill each column, each row, and each of the nine 3 by 3 subgrids that make up a 9 by 9 matrix with the numbers 1 through 9 so that each row, each column, and each subgrid has all of the numbers 1 through 9. For each open spot, given the numbers already in that column, row, and subgrid, there is a set of possible numbers that could go in that spot. If there is only one available number, then great, you are done. But often, your child will have to try putting a number in temporarily. If that number does not work out, your child will have to backtrack and try a different number.

From these examples, we see that search is a general problem-solving method. Your child first identifies all the ways that something could be and then determines which one is the best. We can examine this a little deeper by looking at the old games of Tic-Tac-Toe and Twenty Questions.

Tic-Tac-Toe is a perfect game for introducing a young child to systematic thinking because it is so simple. A child can start to play Tic-Tac-Toe at about four or five years old. Before each move that you or the child makes, count the number of possible moves out loud. For example, before the first move there are nine possible moves. Then after the first move, there are eight possible moves, and so on. For each possible move, say what the opponent would do if that move were made. If you practice this frequently, by the time your child is age six or so, all games should end in a tie.

Twenty Questions is another old game that your child can use to learn about search. In this game, one player thinks of an object, and the other players ask a series of questions to figure out what the object is. The questions asked must have a yes or no answer, and the questions need to determine, of all the possible objects in the universe, which object the player is thinking of. Each question divides the set of all objects into two groups: those that are possibly the object, and those that are not. For example, if you ask whether the object is bigger than a cat and the person says yes, then one group of objects is all the objects in the universe bigger than a cat, and the other group is all the other objects. From this first group, the game continues. The person who correctly guesses the object wins, and if no one can guess the object within twenty questions, the winner is the person who proposed the object.

Twenty Questions uses what computer scientists called *binary search*. The search progresses by breaking the world into two, and then breaking the part of the world that has the object you are looking for into two, and repeating this process until there is only one object left—the one you are looking for. Twenty Questions is a fun game to play in the car. Encourage your child to ask questions that split the set of possible objects into two equal-sized groups. Kids have a tendency to be overly specific in their questions. They will ask something like, "Is it under my bed?" The number of objects under their bed is small, and the number of objects in the rest of the universe is huge. A better question might be, "Is it in the house?" This question makes the balance a little better, and it provides a more even split of the *likely* solutions because of the limitations of experience and how that shapes what objects we think of. If the object is in the house, they should ask if it is on the first floor or second, and continue with questions like this until the object is identified.

Search and Creativity

Creativity is the selection of the *right* possibility from the set of all possibilities. Viewed from this perspective, search *is* creativity.[2] When we think of creativity, we think of an activity like painting a picture or taking an action that is not expected but turns out to be of high quality. When we consider that we are at some state in the world anytime we take an action, we see how creativity aligns with search. The link between creativity and search is easy to see in a game like chess where you can outline all of the next possible moves (or sequences of moves) and choose one that is unexpected and brilliant, but search can also be a framework for understanding domains traditionally thought of as "creative." I mentioned before the idea of all books with fewer than 100,000 words, and we could also think of all poems of fewer than 200 words, where search would be picking the best poems of all those possible poems. Of course, there are too many to consider them all, but we humans excel at using our knowledge about the world to intelligently find the best ones.

The theoretical biologist Stuart Kauffman coined the term "the adjacent possible" to mean everything that is one step away from where you are in the current state space. If you are at the right place, and this is where training and education come in, you can take a leap that no one else has. Big inventions are rarely created from nothing; they more often come into being from a series of small steps through the state space of designs. Incidentally, this is also another reason why scientists try to keep their current questions in their heads all of the time, because you never know when a useful jump might occur to you.

---

[2]I first heard that creativity was search from Professor Gordon Novak in the introduction to artificial intelligence class at the University of Texas at Austin.

Creativity also entails being willing to take jumps that might seem absurd. As we saw in the discussion on humor in Chapter 7, absurd ideas sometimes make surprising sense. Kids are natural explorers of ideas, while adults are more focused on exploiting already-known paths [37]. Adults learn that most options are not useful, so we pick the same ones over and over. This is efficient, but we give up exploration to exploit the knowledge we have already acquired. Teach your child that it is okay to consider unusual possibilities. You don't want to act on every wacky idea that comes into your head, but you want to keep them coming. You never know when a great one might show up.

8.2 Overwhelming Possibilities

One way to gain a deep appreciation for human intelligence is to try to build artificial intelligence embodied in a computer architecture. Computer scientists have been working for decades trying to get computers to do what we do effortlessly, such as recognizing objects in scenes. In this section, we take a deeper look into why it is so hard to build smart computers. This analysis will provide some insight into creativity and how children can be more creative.

Computers lack creativity because they can't effectively individuate concepts to define a usable state space, and they can't search intelligently within a state space because they have limited knowledge. The world is huge, and performing an exhaustive search in a large space is impossible, even for a fast computer. Children can individuate high-level concepts to narrow down the search, and they can use their web of knowledge to decide which actions to take. By contrast, computers have difficulty understanding the layout of a room, they are easily confused by the words that people say, and they don't have the deep commonsense knowledge needed to understand such basic facts such as that a book also moves if the table upon which it is resting is moved. Computers also generally can't understand new situations by analogies to old situations.[3]

Missing Abstractions

The creativity of computers is limited by their inability to see their surroundings at a high level of abstraction. The world is hugely complex, and humans excel at pulling out concepts and patterns from this fire hose of sensory input. Computers are not good at this yet. Consider the task of recognizing a chair in a scene. This is easy for us, but to understand why it is difficult for computers, recall that computers see an image as a huge matrix of numbers. Using this representation means that even for the same chair, if the camera moves an inch to the right, all of the numbers in the matrix corresponding to the chair change. Toddlers see chairs with no problem—it's the sitting still in them that is difficult.

Because computers have difficulty progressing from the low level of numbers to the high level of chairs, computers are not able to fully benefit from the efficiencies of high-level search. Consider writing a story. We write stories by searching through the space of possible ideas and then stringing together a handful of those ideas to make a story. You would never get anywhere if you tried to write

---

[3]See Mitchell [78] for a discussion of computers making analogies.

a story by searching through the space of possible combinations of words because most random combinations of words are meaningless.

The difficulty computers have in recognizing objects is an example of the larger difficulty in recognizing patterns. Interestingly, there have been efforts to trick humans into helping computers recognize patterns. People spend a lot of time playing games, and to harness some of this effort, there are online games that use the power of human pattern recognition to help computers. For example, games like Phylo, Foldit, and Galaxy Zoo use human pattern recognition to help computers do science. In Phylo, players try to find similar regions in genetic sequences. In Foldit, players try to best fold proteins, and players in Galaxy Zoo classify galaxies according to shape.

We even use pattern matching problems to distinguish computers form humans on the Internet. We've all seen that cartoon [97] where a dog is sitting at a computer and turns to another dog and says, "On the Internet, nobody knows you're a dog." While family pets rarely surf the Internet, robots do it all the time, engaging in spam and other mischief. To distinguish humans from robots on the Internet, we exploit their poor pattern recognition capabilities with captchas [106]. Captchas are those annoying pictures of letters that we have to type in to get into a web page. They work because humans can solve them and computers can't. Of course, computers are getting better at recognizing patterns,[4] and there have been ad-

---

[4]You may have heard about *deep learning*. Deep learning is a machine learning method that consists of a large network of simple adaptive functions feeding into one another, loosely organized like neurons in the human brain. Deep learning is currently a hot topic and helps to power Apple's automated personal assistant Siri [47].

vances in object recognition. Automatic teller machines can now read our chicken-scratch handwriting on checks, and captchas are getting so hard that we sometimes have trouble solving them. So the gap is closing, and once computers can identify and represent concepts, they can use the power of their speed. This is why computers are now better chess players than humans. In chess, the models and the features are easy to encode, so the computers can beat us using raw processing power. However, in the real world, computers are still pitiful at understanding their environment compared to toddlers.

Although the pattern recognition capabilities of computers are improving, computers still often cannot make smart choices because they don't have a deep web of knowledge to guide decisions. They do, of course, have the World Wide Web, but they are not very good at making sense of the information on the Internet. Because of this, computers cannot decide which options are not worth pursuing, so they just try everything. In some cases, trying everything can get you surprisingly far. This is a strategy that has been tried by nature, as Lorenz [69] states, "A young corvide bird, confronted with an object it has never seen, runs through practically all of its behavioral patterns, except social and sexual ones."[5] But in the complex world of human culture, computers will need to be smarter than birds.

To provide computers with a web of knowledge, you could feed the computer individual facts, such as that it only rains outside, but there are an infinite number of such things to tell them. For instance, a bird can fly, unless it isn't a flying bird. Well, you could tell the

---

[5]This quote was brought to my attention by Stoytchev in [99].

computer that there are two kinds of birds, those that fly and those that don't. But what if a flying bird is injured and can't fly? You could tell the computer that an injured bird cannot fly. But then, what if the bird is covered in molasses? Kids have had the experience of being covered in heavy things like blankets, and this experience provides them with the common sense to know that even a flying bird cannot fly if it is covered with something heavy like molasses.

Because there is so much to know and because inference is complicated, the hardest part of building smart computers has been teaching them everything that a five-year-old knows. Researchers have tried to just program it in [40, 64], and they have tried to have computers learn domain knowledge for themselves either through low-level primitives [108] or from the Internet [15]. Progress has been slow, but computer intelligence is improving faster than the rate of human evolution, and in the next chapter we will examine the possibility of computers becoming smarter than humans.

We use our deep web of knowledge to make decisions. Even though a toddler tries more actions than does an adult, a toddler still is able to disregard ridiculous possibilities (usually). It is an open question whether or not computers need a physical body to obtain the deep web of knowledge required to understand the world the way that we do. Regardless, computers currently only have a shallow understanding, and this means that they try brute-force search to solve problems. In limited domains, such as chess, this can be successful, but even a child's playroom is far too complex to be understood by looking at *everything*.

Fragmented Memories

For humans, thinking and remembering are intertwined. As we saw in Chapter 5 with Aunt Leona's Juneberry pie, some memories are more accessible than others depending on our current situation. Memories are also linked to each other so that remembering one thing brings to mind all the memories related to it. By contrast, computers have a clear distinction between memory and information processing. This makes certain operations efficient, such as listing all known edible plants.

Within the computer, there might be a table called `Plants` that lists every plant the computer knows about and the different attributes of each plant. One feature for plants in this table could be called `edible`. To generate a list of edible plants, the computer would perform the following operation

```
select plant-name from Plants where
edible = True;
```

While efficient for certain kinds of operations, this table-based representation hurts creativity because all options are always available.[6]

A human will generally only consider the existence of Aunt Leona in situations where the memory of her is likely to be important. By contrast, computers are either always thinking about Aunt Leona or never thinking about her, depending on how their data is organized.

---

[6]There are new representations emerging that more closely resemble the human web of knowledge. These representations are called Linked Data [10] or the Semantic Web [9]. These are exciting technologies, but they are still unfolding.

This means that computers have trouble seeing the relationships between data, unless those relationships are explicitly encoded by programmers. Systematic memory makes computers brittle because when everything seems relevant, nothing is.

Flat Organization

Computers are also brittle because they lack higher-level thought processes. Their knowledge is represented as a bunch of rules: if X then do Y. Computers generally lack higher-level faculties that can look and see when the rules are appropriate or that can change the rules. To be adaptive, computers will need to be able to verify for themselves that what they believe to be true is actually true [100], and they will need to be able to build models about their own thinking. Higher-level, meta structures will enable them to think using metaphors and analogies. As discussed in Chapter 6, analogies are useful for taking what one knows in one domain and applying it to another, and it has been suggested that another way of looking at creativity is to view it as the ability to reason by analogy [41].

1. Systematic, fast, and dumb
2. Brittle
3. Knowledge: small and unconnected
4. Memory: large and unconnected

1. Slow but smart
2. Adaptive
3. Knowledge: large and connected
4. Memory: limited and associative

Figure 8.1: Comparison of computers and humans

Figure 8.1 sums up some of the ways that computers and humans differ. In this chapter, I argued that computers can't think deeply and that they lack the creativity and commonsense reasoning ability of children. In the next chapter we will see how computers are overcoming their limitations with better sensors, better algorithms, and networking. We will also discuss how these advances in computer intelligence are changing the society into which our children are entering.

Tips on Getting Started

Here I provide some tips on helping your child to identify state spaces and search within them.

- Encourage children to identify state spaces—all of the ways in which something can be—and to identify transitions (actions) between states. Examples are all possible next moves in a game.
- When children are stuck solving a problem, encourage them to try all possible actions. This can often help them to get unstuck. For example, if you ask a child if 35 is a prime number, the child may not know (a prime number is a positive whole number that can only be divided evenly by 1 or itself). To solve this problem, ask the child, "Can 35 be divided by 2?" No. By 3? No. By 4? No By 5? Yes! So 35 is not a prime number. Next you can ask your child if 37 is a prime number.
- In addition to teaching your child to exhaustively search a space, teach your child when areas of the state space can be excluded. When determining if 37 is a prime by the method above, you don't have

to go above 19 because $2 \times 19 = 38$, and 38 is greater than 37. So if a number larger than 19 did divide into 37, it would have to go in fewer than 2 times, and there isn't a whole number greater than 1 and less than 2.

Chapter 9

Our Computational Society

Computers are transforming us from an industrial society to a computational one. The transformation is happening at a rapid pace because we are living in a golden age when there is a lack of widespread war, relatively efficient governments in many countries, and global competition that forces companies into a race to make the best product. With little to stop the flow of innovation, computers are getting smaller, sleeker, and more integrated into our lives. The technology is incredible—tablet computers look like something you would find aboard the alien mothership.

Computers still lack the commonsense knowledge possessed by a five-year-old, but there are multiple ways to be intelligent, and computers have been making up for their lack of knowledge by gaining raw processing power and advanced sensors. At some point, we will recognize that the computers all around us have real intelligence.

The truth is that they already do. Each new technology is a useful advance, but it doesn't feel like true intelligence because it is just an incremental improvement over what was there before.

We are already relying on computational technology so much that we are becoming cyborgs with it. Your smartphone knows where you are; it knows how to get you home, and through Google, it has access to just about every fact known to the human race. Your smartphone knows where you should eat; it knows where all of your friends are via GPS tracking, and it knows what all of your friends are doing via status updates. Taken together, this is amazing, but none of the individual pieces—the Internet, online maps, GPS, voice recognition, Google, Facebook—seemed like profound leaps in intelligence.

This chapter will help you teach your child about the computational society in which we live. It is preparation for the next, and final chapter, where I discuss how you can make your child ready to prosper in our new society.

9.1   Intelligent Machines

Computer processing power and memory capacity are growing at an astounding rate. Your smartphone is more powerful than all of the NASA computers that sent astronauts to walk on the moon in 1969 [51]. I remember in 1996 that one gigabyte of hard drive space was a big deal; now the smartphone in my pocket has 16 gigabytes of storage space, and it is the less-expensive version.

IBM has used these improvements in processing power to reach two noteworthy milestones. The first was in chess. We have always viewed chess as an intellectual pursuit, but in 1997, the IBM chess-playing computer Deep Blue beat Garry Kasparov, the best human chess player. At that point, we had to concede that computers were more intellectual in that way needed to excel at chess than humans. But an even greater challenge than chess is the breadth of human culture. Jeopardy! is a game that tests contestant's knowledge of culture through wordplay and puns, and in February 2011, a computer from IBM called Watson beat the two best human Jeopardy! champions.

Both the Jeopardy! and chess challenges were set up so that computers did not have to process information directly from the physical world and were instead reliant on humans to feed them data. With limited sensing abilities, computers can do tasks like tracking business inventories, but only if someone tells them how many items were initially in stock and explicitly notifies them each time an item arrives or is sold. Computers are immensely helpful in this capacity, but recently their sensing capabilities have dramatically expanded, and they can now look out in the world and get information on their own. Computers now use sophisticated algorithms to recognize human speech, recognize faces, read license plates, and even read our sloppy handwriting. Even video games have increased their sensing capabilities. Microsoft's Kinect senses distance and allows you to control video game characters by just moving around your living room.

Robots Running Rampant

With the growing power of computers and sensors, the robot population is increasing. We don't see robots all around us because they don't look like they do in the movies. Instead, robots are currently being used for specialized tasks like vacuuming the floor or welding cars. As technology progresses, the abilities of robots will become increasingly broad, and their numbers will become more visible.

Robots are now fighting in wars, and the trend toward military robots raises difficult questions about who is in charge. Who is to blame when a robot shoots the wrong person? The robot? Currently, there is always a human who makes the decision for the robot to shoot, but these decisions can be affected in subtle ways. In 1988, the American warship USS *Vincennes* shot down an Iranian passenger jet killing 290 civilians, including 66 children, because the computer system aboard the American warship identified the craft as a fighter jet and therefore a threat. Although there was evidence that it was not a fighter jet, the judgment of the computer system influenced the judgment of the humans.[1]

Fighting wars with robots would save the lives of many soldiers, but automation could also lower the cost of conflict and therefore make it more likely. The pilots of drones over Iraq and Afghanistan shoot bad guys, but because they are sitting at a desk in Nevada, they can take their kids to soccer practice when the shift is over.

Robots are also becoming increasingly common in the workplace. In some warehouses, robots are now in charge of moving stock around. When there is an order for a particular item, the robot goes out and gets it and brings it back to the human. These robots are from a company called Kiva Systems (now owned by Amazon.com), and they look like cute, orange, futuristic lawn mowers. They

---

[1]Singer [95] is the source for the section on robots in the military.

pick up racks of items by driving under them.

There are agricultural robots that drive tractors, and in the future they will likely do more complex tasks such as picking oranges. Many companies are working on cars that can drive themselves, and they appear to drive quite well. Once all cars can drive by themselves, we won't need loud sirens on police cars or fire trucks; the emergency vehicles can simply send a radio signal to the cars to give them right of way.

Robots in the home are the most talked-about kind of robots, but they are also the slowest to be developed because our homes are unstructured environments that are hard for a robot to handle. The Roomba robot does the specific task of vacuuming the floor, but household robots are still rare.

Robots don't just hunt terrorists, work in warehouses, and vacuum floors, they also play soccer. Robocup [98] is an international soccer competition with the goal of having a robot soccer team that can beat the best human soccer team by the year 2050. The Sony Aibo robot dogs were primarily used for a number of years and were recently replaced with two-legged robots that are about three feet tall. When you watch them play, you feel simultaneously amazed at what they can do and frustrated by their occasional inability to do the right thing. For me, this is an eerily familiar sensation, because it is the same one I often feel while coaching kindergarten soccer.

The biggest issue surrounding robotics will likely be the loss of jobs caused by automation. To be safe from robot replacement, your child should consider a career that requires a substantial amount of either creativity or manual dexterity, as robots will not be good at either in the near future. Chapter 10 will discuss the skills our children will need for future success.

The Fledgling Computer Collective

Besides getting smarter, computers are starting to talk to each other, and, with our help, they are forming little communities. Smart traffic lights now have the power to enforce their commands. If you run a red light, they take a picture of your license plate and tell the computers that send out tickets to mail one to the person associated with the license plate. The ticket computer then passes the license plate number to the database computer that knows where everyone lives and their license plate number. The database computer then passes back the address, and the ticket computer sends you the ticket.

This type of monitoring is happening everywhere as sensors are increasingly being deployed in the environment. Cameras are watching in restaurants, stores, and intersections all over major cities, and the conversion between our familiar continuous world and the discrete world of symbols used by computers can be done by sophisticated image processing. Not only can computers recognize license plates, they can also recognize your face. We will see in the next chapter how a computer can identify passersby just by looking at their faces. Additionally, there are tollway sensors, GPS chips in cars, RFID sensors (short-distance radio communication), and possibly most important, we increasingly carry around smartphones. These sensors allow computers to link the physical world with the virtual one.

With all these computers watching the world and talking to each other, we are starting to see an Internet of Things [35]. The philosophy behind the Internet of

Things is that the relatively dumb items in our environment will be integrated so that a higher-level intelligence emerges, similar to how even if an ant is not very smart, an ant colony is collectively smart [26]. Consider the simple but profoundly important use case where the Internet of Things lets you know if you forgot your lunch. You could put an RFID on your lunch and on the bag you take in the morning, and you could put a reader on the door. If you were to go through the door with the bag but no lunch, your alarm could sound.

We see little bits of the Internet of Things already as different computers are starting to talk to each other in ways we don't expect. My father-in-law asked me how his new TV knew that his daughter was calling because he saw a message that she was calling flash on his TV screen. The only explanation I could come up with was that the cordless phone broadcasted that there was a call and who it was from, and that broadcast was picked up by the TV (his TV and phone service came from different providers). As another example, my iPhone had my e-mail already there after I docked with iTunes (I had thought that iTunes was just for music). Also, Google Calendar had all my appointments on my Android smartphone. That happened seemingly by magic. And when I type in an address on a map on the desktop, it shows up as a choice on my mobile phone.

The Singularity (The Rapture for the Nerds)

Some authors, such as Vinge [105] and Kurzweil [59], argue that these trends of smarter computers could lead to a point where technology changes so fast that humans can no longer keep up. Programming computers to be smart in a particular domain can take years, but once a computer knows something, it is easy to pass that information along to another computer. Humans require almost 20 years to learn a reasonable amount of what society knows, but a computer could acquire this information in seconds, if another computer already had it.

Computers get smarter every year, while we stay about the same. If this trend continues, their intelligence will surpass our own at some point in the future. The noted futurist Ray Kurzweil believes that this will happen sometime around the year 2045, which for many of us is about the time our children will be the age we are now. This means that we could personally witness the emergence of an alien intelligence that far surpasses our own.

Once computers obtain an intelligence greater than our own, they could create an even greater intelligence, and those computers could create a yet greater intelligence, and so on, leading to what is called *the singularity*. The singularity is a term borrowed from physics. In the center of a black hole, the laws of physics break down and we can't model what is happening there; thus, it is a singularity. The term applies here because we cannot comprehend such a speed of technological change and we have no idea what would happen. Will the computers enslave us? Treat us like pets? Will we merge with them?

The technological singularity seems both impossible and inevitable. Regardless of whether or not it happens, technology will continue to change the world, and our children will need both adaptive and creative thinking to keep up.

9.2 Cybernetic Organisms

Technology is having such a profound effect on humanity and culture that we are now cyborgs living in augmented reality. We've been cyborgs since we began using pencil and paper as memory aids [18]. When calculators and computers came along, we used them to extend our ability to add large numbers and other simple tasks. With the rise of the smartphone and Google, we now have all of the world's knowledge in our front pocket or purse. Our smartphones also store our memories as pictures, movies, and text; and they navigate us to destinations augmented with descriptions and ratings. I am now so used to my smartphone that it seems weird when people ask me for directions, as if an essential component is missing from their brains.

Our Lives in Bits

Geographical distance is no longer a barrier to communication because we now live a large part of our lives in the digital world. The result of this is that the information we exchange between ourselves is now available to computers. Conversations that used to take place in the physical world now take place digitally in places like Facebook or Twitter. Pictures that used to be in albums in the closet are now online on Instagram or Flickr. Not only is our communication data available to computers, it is in a nice, machine-readable form. Photos stored online often have the latitude and longitude coordinates at which they were taken encoded in the image. With Foursquare, we even give important latitude and longitude locations symbolic names such as "Jim Bob's Laundromat," so that we tell the computers how often we do our laundry, and with whom. The result of these trends is that a history of our existence is being stored in computer bits in *the cloud*. The cloud is a trendy name for the Internet, but the focus is more on being a repository for shared information.

One hobby of mine is thinking of strange and unlikely scenarios and wondering if they have ever happened in the history of the planet. For example, has there ever been a cat that rode on the roof of a car all the way to a grocery store? Cats often sit on roofs of cars in driveways, but it is hard to imagine that one would stay on the car when it was started up, and even harder to imagine that one would stay on the car all the way to the grocery store. But, on the other hand, there are lots of cars in driveways and lots of cats, so it's possible that such a thing has happened at least once. Of course, no one cares about cats riding on cars (besides me), but there are serious questions that have a similar nature, and we are starting to collect so much data about the world that we will soon be able to answer such questions. All of this data will allow us to look for correlations in a brute-force way, because even rare events will still happen often enough when you consider the whole planet.[2] These correlations will allow us to do more than ask if a strange event has ever occurred—they will allow us to make predictions and to better understand our world.

Bits in Our Lives

Not only are computers helping us keep track of reality, they are augmenting it. The first mainstream use of augmented reality was the yellow first-down line in NFL football. It is done so well that we just consider it to be

---

[2]Great article about the power of data [38].

part of the experience, and it seamlessly adds to our perception of the physical world. In the future, we will likely wear glasses (such as Google Glass[3]) or contacts that can place information onto the real world just like we see the first-down marker on TV when watching football.

Augmented reality will enrich our experience by laying digital information over everything we see. With augmented reality glasses, we wouldn't need street signs. The glasses could tell us everything we would need to know. We are starting to see augmented reality applications (apps) on the smartphone. There is an app for the iPhone that translates signs in Spanish to English. You point the phone at a sign in Spanish, and it replaces the text on the sign with English text (it also works from English to Spanish).[4] There will also be apps that we can't even imagine now. One of my pet ideas is an app that lets you view the way your town looked 30 years ago.

We saw how augmented reality could make street signs unnecessary and how driverless cars could remove the need for sirens. Broadly, if we could communicate with the right people at the right time, we could reduce the unnecessary broadcasts that add noise and stress to our daily lives. Trains might not need to blow horns that can be heard for miles when crossing a street. Messages could be delivered over smartphones instead of being honked by horns or broadcast over announcements. Airports could go from being loud and stressful places, where we are constantly bombarded with messages for boarding flights that we are not taking, to quiet places where we only get the information we need.

---

[3]http://www.youtube.com/watch?v=9c6W4CCU9M4

[4]Word Lens is the name of the app that translates signs between Spanish and English.

The Global Mind

We saw in Chapter 7 that we are each embodied not only in our own bodies, but in society. Computers are augmenting this societal embodiment by merging our physical and virtual worlds. We leave traces in the virtual world with everything we do. Pictures we post to Twitter and Facebook live forever, and even an old product rating written in anger can show up in surprising places.

All of this interaction between people, the physical world, computers, and the virtual world results in a global mind [53]. The web of knowledge on the Internet (the global mind) is like the web of knowledge in an individual. In the global mind, we are all connected to each other. Data is increasingly being tracked about the state of the world, and computations are being made with that data [4]. If I put an opinion on Facebook or rate a product on Amazon.com, that information is instantly available to everyone else and to all of the computer algorithms looking at the data. I become like a neuron in the global mind. This embedding can lead to a kind of "social search" where the neurons (the people connected to us) might know where a relevant piece of information could be found. You see this all the time on Twitter. People post questions and hope that somebody out there has the answer.

We saw in Chapter 5 that our physical embodiment means that we have limited computational abilities and that our brainpower is a scarce resource. Luckily, the abilities of humans and computers are complementary, and we are just beginning to take advantage of the combination of the complementary abilities of humans and computers and the global mind. Amazon.com does a splendid job of recommending books, and Netflix does well with movies, but I want a recommendation on how to fix my water softener. The computer, through access to the Internet, and through seeing what is going on, could guide me through the repair. Or imagine having Alzheimer's and suddenly finding yourself not remembering how to make coffee. The computer could know what you want to do by knowing your routine and observing where you are standing, and it could direct you through the steps.

To be effective, an application that helps me fix my water softener or make my morning coffee must know more than how to do the tasks, it must know *me*. It must know what I know. If it overestimates what I know, I won't be able to follow the instructions, and if it underestimates what I know, our interactions will be tedious. This is coming—your computer will come to know you through continuous interaction. Your computer will be like a friend.

Tips on Getting Started

Here I provide some tips on helping your child recognize the role of smart computers in the environment.

- Point out the hidden intelligence in the environment. Ask your children how our smartphones know where we are when they give the turn-by-turn directions. Show your children that tollbooths can now read your car's license plates at highway speeds, and show them that automatic teller machines (ATMs) can now read handwritten checks.
- Show your children how advertisers follow you around the web. When you get an ad in your browser that

was triggered by online shopping, or an ad in Gmail triggered by an email you wrote, or an ad in Facebook triggered by a post, show it to your children.

- Show your children how computers can learn about you and make recommendations. You can show them the book recommendations you receive from Amazon.com and the movie recommendations you receive from Netflix. Try to guess with your child why those recommendations were made.

Chapter 10

Preparing Your Child for the Future

The computational future entails new opportunities and new dangers. The labor market will be increasingly competitive due to intelligent computers and international workers who can work via computers. This increased competition will raise the bar on both creativity and productivity. Smart computers will know how to answer your child's questions, but they will also be able to answer everyone else's questions. What will distinguish those who excel from those who don't will no longer be the ability to answer questions, but rather the ability to ask interesting and significant ones.[1]

In addition to facing higher expectations, our children will grow up in front of digital eyes. Social networking sites like Facebook came after most of us parents had gone through the tumultuous period of our early youth,

---

[1] Roger Shank discusses how important it is to ask good questions in [91].

and our thoughts and actions of that time are thankfully beyond the digital event horizon. Our children won't be so lucky; everything that they do online will be stored in a database somewhere, and the collection of databases will not forget and can be used to invade your child's privacy.

Nevertheless, the future will astound us. Computers give our children unprecedented power to create. This power to create was once only held by large organizations filled with anonymous workers, but computer tools bring us back to the age of the artisan where anyone can make something useful. Your child can be like a blacksmith in the Middle Ages, creating anything that can be imagined. This chapter will first discuss how to mitigate the potential dangers of our technological explosion; it will then turn its attention to how to maximize its benefits.

10.1 New Dangers

Increased Competition

The advances in smart computers discussed in the previous chapter will dramatically alter the employment landscape. In the past, new technologies eliminated jobs, but they also created new and better jobs. However, computers are general purpose machines, and this is what makes them a greater threat to jobs than other advances [62]. In fact, as recently as the 1930s, a "computer" wasn't even a thing; it was a job title. A computer was a person who sat in a room and did calculations [54]. The electronic computers that surround us today can do anything that we understand well enough to specify with an algorithm.

We have become used to declining employment in the manufacturing sector, but there will be job losses in the service industry as well [92]. I recently noticed that the Schlotzsky's sandwich restaurant at the Austin airport now has you order using a kiosk instead of talking to a person. You see these self-serve kiosks now at supermarkets and stores everywhere. Marshall Brain [12] describes how industries spanning the spectrum from fast food to transportation may shed millions of jobs. These job losses will come from robots doing physical tasks such as window washing, and from more advanced information processing, so that even lawyers could face job loss [72].

The ability to create artifacts using technology will be a key skill necessary for staying employed in a desirable job. In fact, in the future, if you are not directing computers, they may be directing you. A website called Mechanical Turk (www.mturk.com) allows employers to post tasks for people to complete online such as transcribing audio to text. These tasks generally pay poorly, but it gets worse. Researchers are working on ways to make it easy for the computers themselves to direct humans working on Mechanical Turk [66]. The idea is that if a computer gets a task that it cannot do, it can pay a human a pittance to perform that task in its stead.

Beyond having to compete with increasingly capable and efficient automation, our children will have to compete with humans all over the world. Computers allow work to be done overseas almost as easily as locally, and people in the developing world now have online access to educational materials from elite universities in the United States and Europe. These are wonderful changes for those who currently lack access to education and opportunity, but the employment picture in the developed world may be the most troubling issue of the coming century.

Privacy and Your Child's Data Online

We saw in the previous chapter that our lives are increasingly taking place online. Just about everything that your child does on a computer is tracked in a database somewhere. With the explosion of data being kept, conglomerated portraits of individuals can be put together with surprising detail by linking small scraps of information. The fear is that all of these scraps of information can be put together into a large database that covers information about everyone—a database of ruin [82].

In one famous example, Target identified a teenage girl as being pregnant and sent her pregnancy-related advertising. Her father was enraged and went to the store to complain, stating that his daughter was not pregnant. He later had to apologize because it turned out that she was. Target had learned to identify pregnant people by their shifting purchasing pattern, and it had seen this pattern in his daughter and targeted (no pun intended) her for specific advertising [28].

Children's web surfing is being tracked by large advertising companies so that advertisements can be tailored to them. These companies don't track children specifically, as far as I know, but they do track web users. When you go to a website, you see the site because your browser requests the page. But what isn't obvious is that your browser is not only requesting the page you want, such as www.cnn.com, but also a bunch of other pages of advertising. Each of these pages is sent a cookie (a small file) by your browser that tells them who your are. Then, when you go to another page, such as www.nytimes.com, if any of those ads on the page are placed by the same advertising company as those from www.cnn.com, that company has tracked you from CNN to the *New York Times* site. Social networks, such as Facebook, can also track your surfing through the "Like" button. Even if you don't hit "Like" when you go to a page, Facebook can know that you have been to that web page if you have logged into Facebook within the last month [30].

Tracking isn't necessarily always harmful. While I particularly dislike advertisements because they steal moments of my consciousness, if tracking can be used to target ads to my interests, those moments of thievery might be less painful. However, as we saw in Part II, our behavior is influenced by deep psychological forces, and imagine if marketers could turn those forces against us by observing each of us individually and crafting ads to exploit our weaknesses. What if advertisers learned that your child had a profound fear of snakes? They could use that information to show your child scary advertisements that caused him or her to buy their comforting product. In general, advertisers could identify the technique of persuasion to which each person is most susceptible [14].

Another concern is that small pieces of personal data about us can be put together in surprising ways. It has been shown that a camera watching you in a public place can use facial recognition to link to your Facebook profile and, using information such as your birth date and hometown listed there, can have a reasonable chance at guessing your social security number [1]. This technology could also be deployed to a smartphone application, or even to the wearable glasses introduced in the last chapter, and someone could point the camera at your child and find out information such as likes and dislikes and recent online activity.

Another example of agglomerating individual pieces

of data into a surprising whole comes from location data. Traffic applications use anonymized GPS data from smartphones that give a user's location at a point in time without identifying the user. But even though each point has been anonymized so it does individually identify a user, the points can be put together into paths that belong to individual users and lead to their homes.[2] Yet another example of information leakage comes from photos. We saw in the last chapter that photos often capture the location at which they were taken. If your child takes a picture of your house and posts it online, someone could find out where you live.

Everyone wants your child's data, and your child will give it freely by joining online social networks. Social networking sites encourage us to share demographic information, opinions, likes, and dislikes. It can be easy to give away too much information on these sites, but the dangers of social networking do not mean that your child should stay off the grid. Social networking sites are now important mechanisms in society, and Facebook in particular now serves as an unofficial identity management system.[3] Furthermore, social networks seem to satisfy some kind of primal need to share the little events in our lives. It also feels satisfying to have a permanent record of the jokes and events around us. In a way, online social networks take us back to our village origins when every-

---

[2]Reidentifying a user from anonymous location points comes from Marco Gruteser.

[3]I first heard the idea that Facebook serves as a de facto identity management system from Alessandro Acquisti.

one we cared about was always around.[4] However, your child will need to learn to specify his or her privacy preferences that determine who sees what information, even though this can be difficult.[5] Your child will also need to learn to self-censor what he or she posts because future employers and colleagues are going to see this information too. Marketers will also have this data, and they can use it to not only target ads directly to your child, but also to determine whether your child gets a discount when buying items [4]. Unlike in times past when personal history only existed in people's memories, the Internet doesn't forget.

Some Cautionary Notes about Screen Time

Technology can be great fun, but you don't want your child spending all day staring at a glowing box of pixels. Our web of knowledge is grounded in physical experience, and our natural state is to be out in the sunshine, and there is evidence that too much screen time can lead to attentional problems in young children [16]. Professor Dimitri Christakis at Seattle Children's Hospital hypothesizes that this occurs because the images on TV change too quickly, and this constant change causes the child's brain to adapt and expect that pace of rapid change in the environment. Then, when the child is in a slower environment, such as a classroom, the slow pace causes

---

[4]This idea was noted by Sociologist Zeynep Tufekci in [103], an excellent article on the meaning of social networking. Incidentally, reading this article pushed me over the edge to joining Facebook in 2008.

[5]See Sadeh et al. [90] for research about specifying privacy preferences.

the child stress, and the child wants to move around to increase the rate of stimulation.[6]

Beyond flashing screens, the ubiquity of technology can pose other dangers. Professor Sherry Turkle at the Massachusetts Institute of Technology recently wrote a book about the role of information technology in our lives [104]. She points out that we all need downtime for creativity and to be comfortable with being alone.[7] She also makes the point that consuming technology has never been easier and that this ease of consumption can prevent us from understanding how it actually works. Tablet computers are a great example; the slick interface allows you to use them without understanding the internals. You want to encourage your kids to create, and if all they do is consume media on computers, they are not building new creations.

Overall, you want a balance. We want our children to get the benefits of screen time while minimizing the costs. Consider that it may not be how much TV your children watch, but *what* TV they watch that is important. For instance, PBS shows appear to move more slowly and have decent content, and it seems reasonable that slower-moving shows on stations like PBS would be less damaging. TV can fit into the curiosity cycle, you just need to direct it in productive ways. If your children watch shows about science, they will be interested in science. If they watch Japanese fighting cartoons, they will be interested

---

[6]Web page for Dimitri Christakis `http://www.seattlechildren s.org/medical-staff/Dimitri-A-Christakis/`.

[7]Although, as a counterpoint, I went off the grid for a week when I was in China. I expected that it would clear my mind and enhance my creativity, but I just felt numb and lazy. It reminded me of high school.

in the details of the fighters.

Since parents should limit the time spent with technology in children's early years, try to make the most of the time the child does spend in front of a screen. Have your child watch quality TV and interact with curiosity-promoting computer programs. The best way to do this is to limit what is available. In our house, we only get local TV stations, so the kids are limited to watching fast-paced junk cartoons on Saturday mornings. With full cable, there are always bad choices available, and this can lead to tension. Also, you can buy video games that are curiosity-promoting, as we will see in the next section.

Of course, these steps will only take you so far. Your children will have friends who watch junk, and this will make your children want to watch junk. This is okay— even junk is culture—and you don't want your children to be culturally isolated. Fortunately, by raising your children to be curious about rich and meaningful questions, you will have inoculated them against the worst aspects of our media and consumer culture.

10.2   New Opportunities

Computational tools are now bringing the power to create back to the individual. Children can make movies at home and post them on the Internet, or they can author blogs that are read by people around the world, or they can make and distribute music. Your child can even be a budding designer and dream up fashions and have them fabricated in small batches in China.

This is all possible because the artifacts in our lives are now composed almost entirely of information. As we saw in Chapter 1, prescription drugs have wildly different prices not because of the materials inside, but because of the information they represent. And we saw in Chapter 8 how pictures are now made of pixels of information. The importance of the information content of physical objects is also highlighted by the increasing role of robots in manufacturing, With the right designs, factories of robots can turn out anything, even cars. While our children probably won't immediately be producing automobiles, this shift away from materials toward information represents a significant opportunity. It is no longer necessary to have a factory to create something great—a computer is often all that is needed.

Creation will be how our children are evaluated in school and on the job, because rote operations and regurgitating information will be done by smart computers. This shift in evaluation means that children need to learn a whole new set of skills. They will need to be able to find the right tools, learn how to use them, and improve on existing creations, while giving appropriate credit to the previous work of others. In the workplace, portfolios will no longer be just for graphic designers or other artist types, everyone will have a set of created artifacts that represents who they are and what they can do.

Powerful Tools for Creation

Traditional office software can be fun for your kids in the way that car keys are fun for babies. You can use Microsoft Office or Google Docs as a free alternative. Your children can practice identifying letters using the word processor. To make it fun, make the letters large and colorful. Help your child create presentations with funny pictures and send them to grandparents, aunts, or uncles. You can also use a spreadsheet to do math and to make charts such as bar graphs.

Having powerful electronic tools for creation is not entirely new. I recall being amazed the first time I saw a spreadsheet. In high school, I used to do the books at a pizza place where I worked. One day, the area manager showed me this tool he had created. It seemed like a great leap forward. You just counted the money and typed in the numbers given to you by the cash register in various boxes, and the magic gizmo did the night's books. After that, I had a whole new appreciation for this man. He was no longer just a guy who came around now and then to tell me that I was adding too much cheese to the pizzas—he was a technological wizard. He was a titan of a man. Of course, later I learned in my introduction to computing class that the guy had not created the idea of a spreadsheet, he had simply leveraged the power of an existing tool, and anyone could do it, even me.

In addition to office software, there are also many powerful image manipulation tools, and every kid can now be an amateur photographer. We saw in Chapter 8 that digital pictures are just a bunch of dots of color that our eyes blur together into an image. The old idea that pictures don't lie is now a lie. You can do anything with a picture; you can change the individual dots to change the picture at a low level, you can add or remove objects, you can even make it look like an old photograph. Your children can play with these features and also zoom in on the pictures to see the pixels that they are composed of. Kids can have fun with image manipulation software by changing the colors and making their little brother's face green. One free tool is the powerful image manipulation software called GIMP (see my blog post on getting started with GIMP[8]). Similarly, movies are just sequences of pictures shown rapidly one after the other. With video cameras everywhere today, your child can create movies of their toys and put them on YouTube. Or, for privacy reasons, just send them to relatives.

Computer Programming

In our new world of creation, learning to program allows your child to use the power of computation in the same way that a sorcerer casts spells. When it comes to sorcery, it is hard to beat the programming language Python. I wrote a blog post on getting your child started programming with Python,[9] and there is also a colorful book for teaching kids Python called *Python for Kids* by Jason R. Briggs.

Another way your child can learn programming is through online tutorials. One is called Code Academy,[10] and another great tutorial for learning programming concepts is called Khan Academy.[11] Young children may not be able to do these tutorials by themselves, but you can work through them together. Even if your child does not do full-scale programming, learning the concepts of computer programming will be required to be a literate member of society. Equally important, learning to program teaches the skill of puzzling thing out. Professional pro-

---

[8]http://jonathanmugan.com/blog/2012/07/23/teach-your-child-to-manipulate-images-with-gimp/

[9]http://jonathanmugan.com/blog/2012/11/16/teach-your-child-math-using-programming/

[10]http://www.codecademy.com/

[11]https://www.khanacademy.org/cs/welcome-to-computer-science/882454257

grammers spend a surprisingly large percentage of their time figuring out why their programs don't work. They generate hypotheses, test them, fail, and repeat. In fact, I recently gave the following advice to a co-worker learning to program. It's the process I find myself following every day.[12]

1. Google why it doesn't work.

2. Google all the stuff you didn't understand in the answers to step 1.

3. Randomly try some stuff.

4. Goto 1.

This is the same process we go through when trying to understand just about anything, and experiencing the pain of programming is excellent preparation.

When learning to program and in general, I recommend having a full computer available to your child, not just a tablet. Tablets and smartphones hide the complexity of the operating system so that we can frictionlessly consume content, but they make the *creation* of content difficult. If your home computer or laptop is relatively new, your child can even have his or her own computer within your computer. This computer within a computer is called a *virtual machine*. Your real computer simulates every action of the virtual machine, so it appears just like the computer you normally run. The benefit of a virtual machine is that you don't have to worry about your child letting in a virus or otherwise screwing up your normal computer. If the virtual machine gets messed up, you can

---

[12]This is in a similar vein to the famous XKCD comic `http://xkcd.com/627/`.

just delete it and install another one. See my blog post on getting a virtual machine set up for your child.[13]

Creating Worlds with Video Games

Another great way to create is by designing worlds within video games. Playing video games is fun, but the hard and creative work of defining the game has usually been done by someone else. Someone else has individuated the concepts that will be used in the game and defined how they will interact. There are, however, some games where your child can do the creating. These games allow your child to create worlds and watch them unfold. Your child can design the characters, buildings, and terrain, add music to areas, and apply effects, such as fireworks, to go off in certain places.

One popular game for individual creation is called Minecraft.[14] What is distinctive about Minecraft is the amount of choice available. Most games restrict your possible actions to those that advance a pre-specified narrative. In Minecraft, you can do anything you want, and you can shape the world in any way you desire. The game is completely flexible.

Some games allow children to program interacting, semi-intelligent agents. This mirrors the way the real world is moving, toward agents running amok. Well, hopefully not amok, but where programming was once about writing lines of computer code for a single processor to do a single task, computer programming is now about writing code for an agent to interact with other

---

[13]http://jonathanmugan.com/blog/2012/08/06/computers-all-the-way-down-a-free-virtual-machine-for-your-child/
[14]https://minecraft.net/

agents to get things done. This is precisely the skill that these games teach.

A perfect example of a game where children can create multiple agents is Scratch.[15] Scratch is a free application that allows children to create characters and have them interact. Children can program the behavior of the characters by dragging over little puzzle pieces and putting them together. Your child can come up with novel creations and learn programming along the way. With help, a child could use Scratch from age four or five on. Another example is Alice. Alice is similar to Scratch except that the characters can move in three dimensions instead of two, and the emphasis is more on storytelling.[16] Kodu is a free "visual programming language" for the Xbox 360 and Windows PCs.[17] Kodu is more graphical than Scratch.

Spore is a full-fledged video game that is intended more for entertainment than learning. But in Spore, children can use the amazing interface to create fascinating characters. In the extension, Spore Galactic Adventures, children can also make and play detailed adventures. They can specify the behavior of the characters and how objects interact in the environment, and they can also play games made by others. (Note: Spore is rated 10 and up. There is mating—just a dance—and some of the sounds are violent.) As you advance in the game, there are lots of opportunities for reading, but your child can play before he or she can read. In Spore Galactic Adventures, your child can play games made by others. We have never seen anything weird, but if you are con-

---

[15]http://scratch.mit.edu/
[16]http://www.alice.org/
[17]http://research.microsoft.com/en-us/projects/kodu/

cerned, you might want to turn off the part of playing games made by others.

Your child may prefer playing mindless games, but quality games present a good opportunity to teach by example. If you want him or her to play Scratch, you can sit down and play Scratch, and pretty soon your child will want to play too. By playing these games, children can build up to more advanced programming. After the picture-based programming of Kodu, and the text blocks of Scratch, programming in a standard language like Java or Python should come pretty easily because your child can understand programming language constructs based on analogies to what he or she has learned in these games.

Learning with Graphic Visualizations

Technology has more to offer than games. Graphic illustrations and videos are an engaging and interactive way for your kids to learn about the world. Applications such as Visible Body[18] and Zygote Body (formally Google Body Browser)[19] can help your child visualize what our bones and intestines look like. Also, excellent animated videos about such topics as cells and space can be found on the Internet, and some examples are given at the end of the book.

Maps are another way to teach your child about the world. Maps have gone from being large pieces of paper that were difficult to fold to crowdsourced creations on a computer screen. They are all online at the resolution you desire, and GPS tells you exactly where you are. When you go someplace, have your children locate

---

[18]http://www.visiblebody.com
[19]http://www.zygotebody.com

it on a map such as Google Maps. Your children can find on a map where relatives live and even zoom in to see their houses. Children can see the whole world on their computer screens, an apt description of our future, but it is probably still worth buying a globe. When it comes to conveying topology, there is nothing quite like a 3D model.

Creation and Freedom

Our new culture of creation aligns perfectly with the freedom created by the curiosity cycle. For example, by playing with tools like GIMP, your child will get a glimpse of how special effects are done in movies, and this will lead to incomplete models in the child's mind, stimulating the curiosity cycle. Curiosity is what will be demanded by the marketplace, but more importantly, curiosity offers the possibility for work and play to become indistinguishable. This is a beautiful way to live.

Tips on Getting Started

Here I provide some tips on helping your child interact with the digital world.

- To teach your kids how to sensor themselves on social media, show them the kinds of social media posts that you make. When something funny happens in the house that you want to post, talk about the potential post with them. Discuss the kinds of things that should be posted and the kinds of things that should be kept private.
- Try to balance screen time with physical playtime. Video games are designed to be engaging, and chil-

dren can be sucked in for hours if we let them. Make sure that your children run around in the sunshine of the physical world.

- One problem with video games, and games in general, is that the work of defining the world has already been done by the designer. The players are left with the entertaining and satisfying, but possibly uninteresting, work of searching the remaining space for a solution. We want our children to define worlds, so focus on providing games where your child can create.

- Focus on having children create artifacts like movies, songs, digital characters, and pictures. These artifacts are the virtual counterparts to the pictures on the fridge. Not only do artifacts give your child something to show for his or her efforts, previous artifacts can later be recombined into new ones.

- You want to get your child used to using a fully-functional computer, not just a tablet or smartphone. When you child is three or so, you can open a word processor and make the font really big. You can then have your child start typing in letters. You can put the caps-lock on and make the letters a bright color. Start with showing children how to spell their names. Then move to other fun words such as "MOMMY" or the names of pets.

Conclusion

We make sense of our environment by pulling concepts out of the mass of experience and organizing those concepts into models. Models keep us engaged with the world by allowing us to compare how the world behaves with how the models say it will. Models also allow us to look into the future, and the more concepts and models we have, the better we can predict the future and the richer is our experience. Since these models are also questions about how the world works, they open up new opportunities for learning, and in this way learning feeds on itself, forming the curiosity cycle.

Individuating concepts and learning models allows children to think independently and to not be confined by how other people define the world. The ability to represent the world in new and useful ways is a hallmark of profound intelligence. Many people possess sharp minds and can do impressive calculations to come up with correct answers, but their answers are often beside the point. Curiosity will allow your child to go beyond answering questions to *asking* the right questions, and it will give your child the ability to make inferences beyond the information explicitly given. This adaptive intelligence will enable your child to excel in unexpected situations, whereas those with more brittle thinking will fall back on comfortable thought patterns. In a world dominated by smart computers, curiosity-based thinking will be more valuable than simply coming up with correct answers to given questions.

Independent thinking will also help keep your children safe. We teach children specific techniques to avoid online predators and other dangerous situations, but the bad guys and the world itself are always changing, and children need to be able to evaluate previously unseen situations. Independent thinking and modeling other people's models will be crucial. When crossing the street, your children can consider the driver of the nearby car and make sure that the driver actually sees them before crossing. When your children start to drive, they can constantly be modeling the intentions of the other drivers instead of just reacting. As a common example, if the car ahead of the car in the next lane is slowing down to turn, your children can anticipate that the car behind it may suddenly dart into their lane. In short, your children will be able to predict the future.

Our generation is the last one to grow up in the analog world before the digital revolution of the Internet, and ours is the only generation to be comfortable with both digital and analog living. We know that the Internet didn't come all at once—it came into our lives in waves. We used to check electronic mail, and a few years later, we began to surf the web for the first time. Then we started getting our news and buying books online. A few years after that, we could watch videos—any video ever made—at any time. Following that, our past came back to us with the advent of Facebook. It started out as old high school and college friends, and then it grew to colleagues, neighbors, and Aunt Leona. And recently, all of this came to the phone, and we were no longer ever alone or disconnected, or even lost. Our generation still remembers what it was like to be alone at home on a rainy day or to travel and have little contact with friends and family. By contrast, our children will grow up in a digital world devoid of these experiences.

This new world may result in a population divided into consumers and creators. With the dizzying special effects in animated outlets like movies and video games, your child may be tempted to simply be a consumer. But this environment will also enhance opportunities to create for those with the curiosity and the will. Ultimately, we don't know what direction technology will take us, but we do know that increasingly rapid change is coming. Someday, our kids can explain it all to us, as we sit on the front porch wondering what happened to the good old days.

Useful Media Resources

Videos and Video Series

- *The Way Things Work* An animated series where in each episode a group of people start off with a problem and work to find a solution. Great video series for showing what problem solving is all about—solutions that start off bad but get progressively better.

- http://video.pbs.org/program/off-book/ A set of short videos on technology and art.

- http://www.khanacademy.org/ A whole bunch of great online videos for learning math and science topics covered in elementary school on up.

- http://www.youtube.com/show/cosmicjourneys A series of videos about space.

- http://www.pbs.org/wgbh/nova/sciencenow/ and http://www.pbs.org/wgbh/nova/. High-quality science videos.

- *Roving Mars* Great video about the Mars rovers.

- *Alien Planet* On the Discovery Channel. Excellent video about what it would be like to send a robot probe to another planet.
- Brian Greene, *Space, Time & The Universe* , *The Fabric of the Cosmos*, and *The Elegant Universe*. These Nova videos are the closest thing we have to the answer to life, the universe, and everything.
- Videos about DNA. `http://www.statedclearly.com/list-of-videos-current-and-upcoming/`
- `http://www.youtube.com/watch?v=RrS2uROUjK4` A video about powering cells.
- Great, short explanation of how birds and planes fly. `http://www.youtube.com/watch?v=3So7OMwNgy8&feature=youtube`

Books

- *Teach Your Child to Read in 100 Easy Lessons* by Siegfried Engelmann, Phyllis Haddox, and Elaine Bruner. Effective book for teaching your child to read.
- *Philosophy for Kids: 40 Fun Questions That Help You Wonder About Everything!* by David A. White. A book of fun questions that can start great discussions with your kids. It even has teaching tips to get the most out of the questions.
- *This Book Made Me Do It* by John Woodward. Many neat tidbits for teaching kids new skills for things such as cooking, growing plants, and amazing their friends.
- *Optical Illusions: The Science of Visual Perception* by Al Seckel. Great way to interest your child in perception and how the brain works.

- *Python for Kids* by Jason R. Briggs. In our new world of creation, your child can be a digital sorcerer. This is a comprehensive book for teaching kids to program using a language called Python.

Video Games and Programming

Free games for your children that require creativity:

- **Scratch** allows children to program and make their own games.
- **Alice** allows children to program and tell stories.
- **Kodu** allows children to make games using a graphical language.
- **Phun** is a 2D physics simulator that allows your child to set up a situation and watch it play out.

Board and Card Games

- **Numbers League** is a fun card game for learning addition and subtraction.
  http://www.bentcastle.com/nl.htm
- **Stratego** is great for teaching kids the value of information. You must move to win, but each move also reveals information to the opponent.

Useful Websites

The difficulty with websites, of course, is that sometimes they go dead. However, I wanted to include some links that might be helpful.

- `http://www.mapcrunch.com` Takes you to a random Google image within an area of the world specified by you. Great way to talk about world geography.
- `http://primaxstudio.com/stuff/scale_of_unive rse` A fascinating interactive website for showing how big (and small) things are.
- `http://www.photoshop.com/tools?wf=editor` Your child can upload photos and do simple edits.
- `http://www.codecademy.com/` A site for teaching computer programming. It leads you through exercises.
- Another site for teaching computer programming, aimed at children. `http://www.khanacademy.org /cs/welcome-to-computer-science/882454257`
- `http://madebyevan.com/webgl-water/` Cool simulation of water. Explain to your children that the physical world can be simulated on computers.

Podcasts and Other

- *The Math Dude* podcast. He explains math starting from the beginning.
  `http://mathdude.quickanddirtytips.com/`
- If your child likes comic books, here is one about synthetic biology `http://web.mit.edu/endy/www/ scraps/comic/AiSB.vol1.pdf`.

The Curiosity Cycle and Research in Developmental Robotics

Current robots are brittle and uncreative. One theory is that they have these deficiencies because they can't learn on their own the way human children do [108]. My research in developmental robotics was focused on trying to answer the question of how robots could learn by autonomous experience in the environment. We know that children learn by trying things out and exploring, and it seems like it would be easy to replicate that on a robot—just have the robot try a bunch of things and learn what works and what doesn't. For instance, if the robot's hand is to the left of the block, and it moves its hand to the right, the robot should notice that the block also moves to the right. The robot should be able to learn about the world by keeping track of all such learned contingencies. However, this approach is surprisingly challenging.

Robot eyes consist of video cameras that receive millions of pixel values per second. These pixels are an un-interpreted mess. Humans effortlessly understand scenes in the environment; we figure out what is important and what should be ignored, and we decide which things are related to which other things. This all happens subconsciously, and we don't realize how much processing is required. Moving around in the world is also surprisingly challenging. A robot only has access to low-level motors that it must set many times a second. We humans move effortlessly and gracefully without realizing how hard it is. A high-level action like picking up an object can take hundreds or thousands of little decisions. How can a robot learn high-level actions and high-level concepts from these low-level pixels and motors?

To get a foothold on the problem of perception, a robot can identify objects that move by grouping together blobs of changing pixels. By tracking these blobs, the robot has access to the locations of objects such as its hand or blocks in the world. The robot can define variables for the locations of the center and the edges of a blob to indicate where objects are and where they are relative to each other. But even this smaller input is still a mess. Instead of having a bunch of pixels, the robot now has a bunch of variables. How can it start to make sense of all these variables?

The robot can start to make sense of the variables by breaking their continuous values up into a finite set of discrete values. For instance, if there was a variable for temperature, the infinite number of possible temperatures could be broken into five possible values: below freezing, at freezing, liquid water, at boiling, and boiling. In this case, both "at freezing" with a value of 32°F and "at boiling" with a value of 212°F are special because there are semantically meaningful transitions in the environment at these points. We call these important points *landmarks* [57].

The robot can begin with a very small set of landmarks. The robot can then take the landmarks it knows and start to build a bunch of simple, unreliable models to describe small parts of the environment. Then, for each model, it can see if there is some new landmark that could be found on a variable that would make that model more reliable. For example, the robot could have a model that says that if it walks on a wet surface, it will slip and fall. This model may not always hold; sometimes its little robot feet might get wet, but the robot does not fall. By looking at the value of the temperature variable for each experiment, the robot could notice that there is a distinction between the temperature when it falls and when it doesn't. Most of the times when the robot falls, the temperature is below 32°F, and most of the times when it doesn't fall, the temperature is above 32°F. The robot could then create a landmark for the temperature being 32°F, and it would now have a new way to see the world. This new distinction would enable the robot to learn new models that it couldn't learn before. For example, using this landmark, the robot could easily predict when it is going to snow compared to when it is going to rain.

As with the curiosity cycle described in Part I, the robot will be constantly building models, testing them, and looking for new landmarks. Each model will only be about a small part of the world, and some parts of the world may have multiple models. The robot will learn when to use each model for each situation.

In addition to learning how to understand the world through landmarks and models, the robot must also learn how to perform high-level actions. An action is a way to purposefully change the world to some desired state. To learn actions, the robot can use the learned models. Each learned model predicts how some small part of the world will change. This means that once models are learned, they can be composed together to form actions. Higher-level actions can be built upon lower-level actions to form a hierarchy. The robot can then think in terms of these higher-level actions and consider the ones lower on the hierarchy to be automatic. The combination of higher-level actions and landmarks helps to solve the problem of it taking so many little decisions to complete an action. The higher-level actions abstract away all of the little decisions, and the landmarks give the robot values to shoot for. It can think things like, "I need to move my hand to the left until it is over the block." Depending on where the hand currently is, such an action could take over 100 small movements. This interleaving of landmarks, models, and actions is the web of knowledge of the robot.

To maximize learning, the robot needs to explore the world effectively. New actions allow the robot to change the environment in ways it could not before. Low-level exploration using random movements will not lead to effective actions any faster than writing a 100,000 word book using random words will lead to a good book. Clearly, the robot needs to explore in the space of higher-level actions.

The robot learns landmarks, models, and actions all at the same time while exploring the world. But even in this smaller space of learned actions, efficient learning requires more than choosing actions randomly. Some actions would be too easy, and practicing them would be a waste of time. Likewise, some actions would be too hard and also a waste. The best thing to do is for the robot to explore where it is making learning progress [84]. The robot measures how well it can do an action and keeps practicing it until it is perfected, or until it hits a plateau and stops improving.

A robot built on these principles was tested using a physics simulator. Physics simulators are amazing tools that allow you to create a world with gravity, collisions, momentum, everything—without having to worry about burning out motors on a physical robot. In this world, there was a robot sitting at a table with a simple arm and a block (or two) on the table and two floating background objects that the robot could perceive but could not interact with. The variables were specified for the environment such as the location of objects relative to the robot and each other. In this environment, the robot wakes up to the "blooming, buzzing confusion" [44] of all of the values of the uninterpreted variables without any idea as to what they mean. The robot then begins to autonomously explore the world. (See the video http://videolectures.net/aaai2010_mugan_qlap/.)

The robot learns entirely on its own. In most developmental trajectories, the robot first learns to control its hand and move it relative to itself and the block. The robot then learns that it can manipulate the block. In the process of learning how to hit the block, the robot learns that if its hand is on the left side of the block and it moves its hand to the right, the block will also go to the right. This is interesting because initially the robot has no concept of "the left side of the block." By learning the appropriate landmarks, the robot learns that there is such a thing as having its hand on the left side of the block, and this new concept allows it to map the infinite number of possible states where its hand is on the left to a single state. Before knowing what it means to have the hand on the left side of the block, each instance looks different—the robot cannot generalize. But after learning that landmark, it can map all of those instances to a single state. By learning to hit the block, the robot has learned to see the world in a more useful way.

The robot also learns other actions such as picking up a block using a magnetic hand. It is noteworthy that you can't necessarily predict how the robot is going to perform a task. The robot learns many small models and many ways to perform actions, and this gives the robot adaptive thought. During its development, the robot generally learns to move the block left, right, and forward. But it may not prefer to move the block each direction by pushing. In one case, it learned to pick up the block to move it left or right, but it pushed the block to move it forward. Often while you watch the robot, you see it trying different ways to perform an action, and sometimes it has trouble, and then it is wonderful to see it finally succeed.

In experiments, the robot was able to learn in the presence of distractor objects. Learning was not inhibited by the distractor objects because in the developmental process, the robot learns based on what is possible. It doesn't try to understand the whole world, just what it needs for its particular goal. The traditional learning algorithm we compared it to was not able to determine which parts of the world were worth paying attention to. By contrast, our robot learned what was important as an integral part of its development. What was important to the robot was what was predictable or could be used to help predict something else. Using this idea of predictability, the robot even learns what is part of "self" based on what it can reliably control with low latency.

Researchers around the world are working on this problem of enabling robots to learn the way that human children do. Progress has been slow, and most robots you will encounter will have been programmed to do particular tasks, which stands in contrast to the developmental learning approach presented here. Many current and near-term robots will incorporate a limited form of learning such as how to pick up different types of objects, but future robots will rely on increasingly broad learning to acquire skills. The idea of intelligent robots can be scary, and that is why it is so interesting to watch movies about the Terminator scenario. With any advanced technology, we can't assume that there are no risks, but it is fascinating to consider what we can learn about learning and about ourselves by building intelligent robots. Someday, they might even help us solve some of our most challenging problems.

Acknowledgments

I would like to thank my wife Monica and my children Noah, Nathan, and Neala for putting up with the time I spent writing this book. I would also like to thank my parents for their love and support. My mom also provided valuable comments on earlier drafts. My sister Kim Ohman and old classmate Katy Harper Siewert took the time to read an earlier draft and provided helpful comments. I also thank Thayne Coffman, Matthew McClain, and Abbey McGrew for their valuable comments on an earlier draft of this second edition.

Roberto Weber helped me to improve my writing in college, and my Ph.D. thesis advisor Benjamin Kuipers taught me how to investigate and present ideas. Val Toch designed the cover. Editor Lynne Stair provided edits that not only improved the book but also taught me much about writing. Thank you all.

Terms and Definitions

analogy Like a metaphor, an analogy uses one understood idea to give meaning to another idea that is less understood.

articulate To define the exact edges of a concept or model. Often, a concept or model feels fully formed in our head when, in reality, it is only half formed. Articulation is the process of clearly defining what a concept or model is. Communicating ideas to another person is often a great way to force yourself to articulate a concept or model.

brittle thinking Thinking that relies on established patterns and rote memorization. The opposite of adaptive thinking.

concept Something a person can pull out of the mass of experience. It can be a person, place, thing, or idea. A chair is a concept. Talking loudly is a concept. Color is a concept. A concept can also be a feature of something, such as "large" or "round" or "loud" or "heavy." A concept can also be a category, such as "dog" is a category of "animal."

curiosity cycle The learning process that consists of individuating concepts, using those concepts to build models, and testing models. We all have multiple curiosity cycles going at once, and the product of these curiosity cycles is a web of knowledge. Natural curiosity makes the cycles go around, and the cycles also add to curiosity.

deep knowledge Knowledge that is embedded in the web of knowledge.

embodiment A phenomenon is embodied when it is implemented in a particular architecture. The nature of this architecture determines which tasks are easy and which tasks are hard. Human intelligence is implemented in the brain, and machine intelligence is implemented in computers.

grounded knowledge A synonym for deep knowledge. The use of the term "grounded" highlights that the web of knowledge is tied to the physical world and our physical bodies.

incomplete model A model that does not perfectly predict the environment. Almost all models are incomplete. Incomplete models spur curiosity.

individuate To pull a cohesive piece out of the continuous whole of experience. When you see a particular tree in the mass of a forest, you have individuated that tree.

metaphor Something that points to or gives meaning to something else. We understand abstract concepts through metaphors to physical experience. For example, "love is war."

model A linking of concepts. Models can be used to predict the future, such as predicting that a certain person will do well on an exam. Models can be causal models that show how the world changes, or they can be observed patterns that predict the future but the learner does not understand why.

pattern A recurring theme in the environment. A pattern is like a concept because you can individuate it. A pattern is also a model because it can be used for prediction.

state space All of the ways the world can be (or at least a part of the world that you care about).

web of knowledge Knowledge that a person has about the world that is all linked together. Each piece of knowledge is connected to other pieces of knowledge, creating a web.

Bibliography

[1] A. Acquisti, R. Gross, and F. Stutzman. Faces of Facebook—or, how the largest real ID database in the world came to be. In *Black Hat*, 2011.

[2] D. Ariely and S. Jones. *Predictably Irrational: The Hidden Forces That Shape Our Decisions.* Harper New York, 2008.

[3] S. E. Asch. Opinions and social pressure. *People and Productivity*, pages 335–342, 1969.

[4] S. Baker. *The Numerati.* Houghton Mifflin Harcourt, 2008.

[5] D. H. Ballard. Animate vision. *Artificial Intelligence*, 48:57–86, 1991.

[6] A. Bandura. *Self-Efficacy in Changing Societies.* Cambridge University Press, 1995.

[7] R. T. Benjamin, J. R. Hopkins, and J. R. Nation. *Psychology.* Macmillan Publishing Company, 1990.

[8] L. E. Berk. *Infants, Children, and Adolescents.* Allyn and Bacon, 1993.

[9]   T. Berners-Lee, J. Hendler, and O. Lassila. The semantic web. *Scientific American*, 284(5):28–37, 2001.

[10]   C. Bizer, T. Heath, and T. Berners-Lee. Linked data-the story so far. *International Journal on Semantic Web and Information Systems (IJSWIS)*, 5(3):1–22, 2009.

[11]   G. Blanke. How to think faster, better on your feet. CNN, `http://www.cnn.com/2008/LIVING/08/12/rs.how.to.think.on.feet/index.html`, 2008. Accessed on 8/4/2013.

[12]   M. Brain. Robotic nation. `http://marshallbrain.com/robotic-nation.htm`, 2003.

[13]   J. M. Burger and A. L. Lynn. Superstitious behavior among American and Japanese professional baseball players. *Basic and Applied Social Psychology*, 27(1):71–76, 2005.

[14]   R. Calo. Why opt out of tracking? Here's a reason. The Center for Internet and Society, Stanford Law School, August 2013. `http://cyberlaw.stanford.edu/blog/2013/08/why-opt-out-tracking-heres-reason` Accessed on 9/6/2013.

[15]   A. Carlson, J. Betteridge, B. Kisiel, B. Settles, E. R. Hruschka Jr., and T. M. Mitchell. Toward an architecture for never-ending language learning. In *Proceedings of the Twenty-Fourth Conference on Artificial Intelligence (AAAI 2010)*, 2010.

[16] D. A. Christakis, F. J.J. Zimmerman, D. L. DiGiuseppe, and C. A. McCarty. Early television exposure and subsequent attentional problems in children. *Pediatrics*, 113(4):708, 2004.

[17] S. Chritchley. What is a philosopher? New York Times, http://opinionator.blogs.nytimes. com/2010/05/16/what-is-a-philosopher, May 2010. Accessed on 8/17/2013.

[18] A. Clark. Natural-born cyborgs? In J. Brockman, editor, *Science at the Edge: Conversations with the Leading Scientific Thinkers of Today*. Union Square Pr, 2008.

[19] S. C. Cloninger. *Theories of personality: understanding persons*. Prentice Hall, 1993.

[20] L. B. Cohen, H. H. Chaput, and C. H. Cashon. A constructivist model of infant cognition. *Cognitive Development*, 17:1323–1343, 2002.

[21] D. Coon and J. O. Mitterer. *Introduction to Psychology: Gateways to Mind and Behavior*. Wadsworth Pub Co, 2008.

[22] L. F. Cranor. How to foil "phishing" scams. *Scientific American*, 105(104), 2008.

[23] M. Csikszentmihalyi. *Flow: The Psychology of Optimal Experience*. Harper & Row, New York, 1990.

[24] J. Davis. Pissing match: Is the world ready for the waterless urinal? Wired, http://www.wired.com/magazine/2010/06/ff_waterless_urinal/, June 2010. Accessed on 8/4/2013.

[25] A. J. DeCasper and A. Carstens. Contingencies of stimulation: Effects of learning and emotions in neonates. *Infant Behavior and Development*, 4:19–35, 1981.

[26] M. Dorigo and T. Stützle. *Ant Colony Optimization*. The MIT Press, 2004.

[27] G. L. Drescher. *Made-Up Minds: A Constructivist Approach to Artificial Intelligence*. MIT Press, Cambridge, MA, 1991.

[28] C. Duhigg. How companies learn your secrets. New York Times, http://www.nytimes.com/2012/02/19/magazine/shopping-habits.html, February 2012. Accessed on 6/3/2013.

[29] C. Dweck. The secret to raising smart kids. *Scientific American Mind*, 18(6):36–43, 2007.

[30] A. Efrati. 'Like' button follows web users. Wall Street Journal, http://online.wsj.com/article/SB10001424052748704281504576329441432995616.html, May 2011. Accessed on 8/4/2013.

[31] S. Engelmann, P. Haddox, and E. Bruner. *Teach Your Child to Read in 100 Easy Lessons*. Fireside, 1986.

[32] S. Freud. *The Ego and the Id*. The Hogarth Press Ltd., 1949 (Original work published 1923).

[33] B. Gelpke, R. McCormack, and R. Caduff. *A Crude Awakening: The Oil Crash*. Lava Productions, AG, 2006.

[34] G. Gergely and J. S. Watson. Early socio-emotional development: Contingency perception and the social-biofeedback model. *Early social cognition: Understanding others in the first months of life*, pages 101–136, 1999.

[35] N. Gershenfeld, R. Krikorian, and D. Cohen. The internet of things. *Scientific American*, 291(4):76–81, 2004.

[36] D. T. Gilbert. *Stumbling on Happiness*. Knopf, 2006.

[37] A. Gopnik. *The Philosophical Baby: What Children's Minds Tell Us About Truth, love, and the meaning of life*. Farrar Straus & Giroux, 2009.

[38] A. Halevy, P. Norvig, and F. Pereira. The unreasonable effectiveness of data. *Intelligent Systems, IEEE*, 24(2):8–12, 2009.

[39] C. Haney, W. C. Banks, and P. G. Zimbardo. Study of prisoners and guards in a simulated prison. *Naval Research Reviews*, 9:1–17, 1973. http://www.zimbardo.com/downloads/1973%20A %20Study%20of%20Prisoners%20and%20Guard s,%20Naval%20Research%20Reviews.pdf.

[40] D. Hart and B. Goertzel. Opencog: A software framework for integrative artificial general intelligence. In *Artificial General Intelligence, 2008: Proceedings of the First AGI Conference*, page 468. Ios Pr Inc, 2008.

[41] J. Hawkins and S. Blakeslee. *On Intelligence*. Owl Books, 2005.

[42] W. F. Hill. *Learning: A Survey of Psychological Interpretations.* HarperCollins, 1990.

[43] T. Hobbes and M. J. Oakeshott. *Leviathan, or, The Matter, Forme and Power of a Commonwealth Ecclesiasticall and Civil.* Touchstone, 1997.

[44] W. James. *The Principles of Psychology.* Harvard University Press, Cambridge, MA, 1981. Originally published in 1890.

[45] M. Johnson. *The Body in the Mind: The Bodily Basis of Meaning, Imagination, and Reason.* University of Chicago Press, Chicago, Illinois, USA, 1987.

[46] S. J. Johnson and A Corn. Screen assessment for gifted elementary students [kit], 1987.

[47] N. Jones. Computer science: The learning machines. Nature, News Feature, http://www.nature.com/news/computer-science-the-learning-machines-1.14481, January 2014. Accessed on 3/9/2014.

[48] D. Kahneman. Maps of bounded rationality: Psychology for behavioral economics. *American Economic Review*, 93(5):1449–1475, 2003.

[49] D. Kahneman. *Thinking, fast and slow.* Farrar, Straus and Giroux, 2011.

[50] D. Kahneman, P. Slovic, and A. Tversky. *Judgment under Uncertainty: Heuristics and Biases.* Cambridge University Press, 1982.

[51] M. Kaku. *Physics of the Future: How Science Will Shape Human Destiny and Our Daily Lives by the Year 2100.* Doubleday, 2011.

[52] K. Kelly. *Out of Control: The New Biology of Machines, Social Systems and the Economic World,* volume 474. Addison-Wesley, 1994.

[53] K. Kelly. *What Technology Wants.* Viking Penguin, 2010.

[54] P. Kennedy. Mind and machine, part 1. CBN Radio One, September 2013.

[55] S. King. *On writing.* Simon and Schuster, 2002.

[56] C. Krauss and E. Malkin. Mexico oil politics keeps riches just out of reach. New York Times, http://www.nytimes.com/2010/03/09/bu siness/global/09pemex.html, March 2010. Accessed on 8/4/2013.

[57] B. Kuipers. *Qualitative Reasoning.* The MIT Press, Cambridge, Massachusetts, 1994.

[58] J. H. Kunstler. *The Long Emergency: Surviving the End of Oil, Climate Change, and Other Converging Catastrophes of the Twenty-first Century.* Grove Pr, 2006.

[59] R. Kurzweil. *The Singularity Is Near.* Penguin books, 2005.

[60] G. Lakoff and M. Johnson. *Metaphors We Live By.* University of Chicago Press, Chicago, 1980.

[61] G. Lakoff and R. E. Núñez. *Where mathematics comes from: How the embodied mind brings mathematics into being.* Basic Books, 2000.

[62] T. Lane. The rise of our robot overlords. `http://cs.unm.edu/~terran/academic_blo g/?p=151`, January 2013.

[63] M. D. Lemonick and J. M. Nash. Cosmic conundrum. The universe seems uncannily well suited to the existence of life. Could that really be an accident? *Time*, 164(22):58, 2004.

[64] D. B. Lenat. CYC: A large-scale investment in knowledge infrastructure. *Communications of the ACM*, 38(11):33–38, 1995.

[65] S. D. Levitt and S. J. Dubner. *Freakonomics: A Rogue Economist Explores the Hidden Side of Everything.* William Morrow & Co, 2005.

[66] G. Little, L. B. Chilton, M. Goldman, and R. C. Miller. Turkit: human computation algorithms on Mechanical Turk. In *Proceedings of the 23nd annual ACM symposium on User interface software and technology*, pages 57–66. ACM, 2010.

[67] P. Lockhart. *Measurement.* Harvard University Press, 2012.

[68] G. Loewenstein. Out of control: Visceral influences on behavior. *Organizational Behavior and Human Decision Processes*, 65(3):272–292, 1996.

[69] K. Lorenz. Innate bases of learning. In K.H. Pribram and J. King, editors, *Learning as Self-*

Organization, Inns Series of Texts, Monographs and Proceedings Series. L. Erlbaum Associates, 1996.

[70] J. Mandler. *The Foundations of Mind, Origins of Conceptual Thought.* Oxford University Press, New York, New York, USA, 2004.

[71] G. F. Marcus. *Kluge: The Haphazard Construction of the Human Mind.* Houghton Mifflin Harcourt, 2008.

[72] J. Markoff. Armies of expensive lawyers, replaced by cheaper software. New York Times, http://www.nytimes.com/2011/03/05/sc ience/05legal.html, March 2011. Accessed on 8/4/2013.

[73] M. W. Matlin. *Cognition.* Harcourt Brace Publishers, 1994.

[74] S. Milgram. *Obedience to authority: An experimental view.* Harper & Row (New York), 1974.

[75] C. C. Miller. Data science: The numbers of our lives. New York Times, http://www.nytimes.com/2013/04/14/educat ion/edlife/universities-offer-courses-i n-a-hot-new-field-data-science.html, April 2013. Accessed on 8/2/2013.

[76] G. A. Miller. The magical number seven, plus or minus two: some limits on our capacity for processing information. *Psychological Review*, 63(2):81, 1956.

[77] W. Mischel, Y. Shoda, and M. I. Rodriguez. Delay of gratification in children. *Science*, 244(4907):933, 1989.

[78] M. Mitchell. *Complexity: A Guided Tour.* Oxford University Press, USA, 2009.

[79] T. E. Moffitt, L. Arseneault, D. Belsky, N. Dickson, R. J. Hancox, H. L. Harrington, R. Houts, R. Poulton, B. W. Roberts, S. Ross, M. R. Sears, W. M. Thomson, and A. Caspi. A gradient of childhood self-control predicts health, wealth, and public safety. *Proceedings of the National Academy of Sciences*, 108(7):2693, 2011.

[80] D. G. Myers and H. Lamm. The group polarization phenomenon. *Psychological Bulletin*, 83(4):602, 1976.

[81] T. E . Nelson, Z. M. Oxley, and R. A. Clawson. Toward a psychology of framing effects. *Political Behavior*, 19(3):221–246, 1997.

[82] P. Ohm. Broken promises of privacy: Responding to the surprising failure of anonymization. *UCLA Law Review*, 57:1701, 2010.

[83] P. Y. Oudeyer and F. Kaplan. How can we define intrinsic motivation? In *Proceedings of the International Conference on Epigenetic Robotics*, 2008.

[84] P. Y. Oudeyer, F. Kaplan, and V. V. Hafner. Intrinsic motivation systems for autonomous mental development. *Evolutionary Computation, IEEE Transactions on*, 11(2):265–286, 2007.

[85] R. Penrose and M. Gardner. *The Emperor's New Mind*, volume 364. Citeseer, 1999.

[86] D. T. Phillips. *Run to Win: Vince Lombardi on Coaching and Leadership.* St. Martin's Griffin, 2002.

[87] J. Piaget. *The Origins of Intelligence in Children.* Norton, New York, 1952.

[88] R. M. Pirsig. *Zen and the Art of Motorcycle Maintenance.* Bodley Head, 1974.

[89] E. A. Plant, K. A. Ericsson, L. Hill, and K. Asberg. Why study time does not predict grade point average across college students: Implications of deliberate practice for academic performance. *Contemporary Educational Psychology*, 30(1):96–116, 2005.

[90] N. Sadeh, J. Hong, L. Cranor, I. Fette, P. Kelley, M. Prabaker, and J. Rao. Understanding and capturing people's privacy policies in a mobile social networking application. *Personal and Ubiquitous Computing*, 13(6):401–412, 2009.

[91] R. C. Schank. Are we going to get smarter? In J. Brockman, editor, *The Next Fifty Years: Science in the First Half of the Twenty-first Century.* Vintage, 2002.

[92] A. Semuels. Retail jobs are disappearing as shoppers adjust to self-service. Los Angeles Times, http://articles.latimes.com/2011/mar/04/bu siness/la-fi-robot-retail-20110304, March 2011. Accessed on 8/4/2013.

[93] R. A. Serway, R. J. Beichner, J. W. Jewett, and J. R. Gordon. *Physics for Scientists and Engineers*, volume 1. Saunders College Publishing, 2000.

[94] H. A. Simon. *The Sciences of the Artificial*. The MIT Press, 1996.

[95] P. W. Singer. *Wired for War*. Penguin Press, 2009.

[96] R. C. Solomon. *The Passions: Philosophy and the Intelligence of Emotions*. The Teaching Company, 2006.

[97] P. Steiner. On the internet, nobody knows you're a dog. The New Yorker, July 1993.

[98] P. Stone. Intelligent autonomous robotics: A robot soccer case study. *Synthesis Lectures on Artificial Intelligence and Machine Learning*, 1(1):1–155, 2007.

[99] A. Stoytchev. Toward learning the binding affordances of objects: A behavior-grounded approach. In *Proceedings of AAAI Symposium on Developmental Robotics*, pages 17–22, 2005.

[100] A. Stoytchev. Some basic principles of developmental robotics. *Autonomous Mental Development, IEEE Transactions on*, 1(2):122–130, 2009.

[101] S. Strogatz. *The Joy of X: A Guided Tour of Mathematics, from One to Infinity*. Houghton Mifflin Harcourt, 2012.

[102] R. H. Thaler and C. R. Sunstein. *Nudge: Improving Decisions about Health, Wealth, and Happiness*. Yale University Press, 2008.

[103] C. Thompson. New york times, brave new world of digital intimacy. http://www.nytimes.com/2008/

`09/07/magazine/07awareness-t.html`, September 2008. Accessed on 1/4/2014.

[104] S. Turkle. *Alone Together: Why We Expect More from Technology and Less from Each Other.* Basic Books, 2011.

[105] V. Vinge. The coming technological singularity. *Whole Earth Review*, pages 88–95, 1993.

[106] L. Von Ahn, M. Blum, and J. Langford. Telling humans and computers apart automatically. *Communications of the ACM*, 47(2):56–60, 2004.

[107] R. A. Weber. 'Learning' with no feedback in a competitive guessing game. *Games and Economic Behavior*, 44(1):134–144, 2003.

[108] J. Weng, J. McClelland, A. Pentland, O. Sporns, I. Stockman, M. Sur, and E. Thelen. Autonomous mental development by robots and animals. *Science*, 291:599–600, 2001.

[109] E. P. Wigner. The unreasonable effectiveness of mathematics in the natural sciences. *Communications on pure and applied mathematics*, 13(1):1–14, 1960.

[110] D. Zarefsky. *Argumentation: The Study of Effective Reasoning.* The Teaching Company, 2001.

Index

23223372R00125

Printed in Great Britain
by Amazon